CONTENTS

Introduction 5

Prehistoric Britain 7

Rotten Roman Britain 12

Invading Brits 18

Dreadful Dark-Age Britain 24

Nasty Norman Britain 28

Sporty Brits 34

Measly Middle-Age Britain 38

Terrible Tudor Times 46

Noshing Brits 52

Slimy Stuart Times 56

Gory Georgian Britain 62

Criminal Brits 68

Vicious Victorian Britain 73

Working Brits 78

The Terrible 20th Century 84

Epilogue 88

Great British Losers 89

Interesting Index 95

INTRODUCTION

What's Britain? Three countries sharing one island in the north-west corner of Europe. England, Scotland and Wales. Add another horrible island called Ireland and you have the 'British Isles'.

Some of the most horrible history in the world has taken place on those little islands.

From time to time the four countries have had some savage squabbles.

Take England – the country of St George, the man who is remembered for killing a people-eating dragon.

England has more people than the other three put together – so that has made it the biggest bully.

But in this book England only comes first because it is first in the *alphabet* ... not because it's most important.

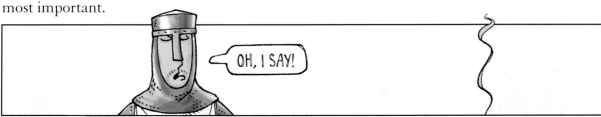

Ireland comes next ... in the alphabet. The land of St Patrick, who taught the Christian religion to the Irish. The island of Ireland has no snakes ... probably because it rains a lot and the soaked snakes slithered into the sunset.

Hmmmm! Believe that if you want.

Third we have Scotland. A land of warriors, mountains and castles. The country of St Andrew, a fisherman and friend of Jesus who was executed – tied to a cross. That was a slower way to die than being nailed. He preached for two days before he died…

Fourth we have Wales. A land of dragons and daffodils. The land of St David … a holy man and a monk. He taught the Welsh soldiers to wear leek plants in their hats so they knew who was on their side in battle. They must have looked real twits.

If you want to understand who these curious people were then you need a history to tell you all the deadly details.

A horrible history. Where shall we start…?

PREHISTORIC BRITAIN

It's amazing how long people have been wandering around the British Isles. It started so long ago it was 'pre-historic' ... that is 'before history lessons'. It was even before history teachers. They weren't invented till around 3000 BC. Here are a few dates.[1]

TERRIBLE TIMELINE

300,000 BC
Britain is joined to France, so early humans (Homo erectus) wander across. They hunt for mammoths and hippos in southern England. No wonder you don't see hippos there today. The cavemen killed them!

70,000 BC
Neanderthals (another type of human) come across. They will be extinct by 35,000 BC. Dead as a dinosaur's toenail.

12,000 BC
Modern humans arrive from Europe. The end of the ice age and goodbye to frozen pees. Nicer weather but it's not all good news - it will be another 13,900 years before anyone invents fridges and frozen peas.

8000 BC
Humans arrive in Ireland to hunt and fish. But they do not open fish shops because chips haven't been invented yet.

7500 BC
Oh, no! The English Channel floods and cuts off Europe. Those poor people on the continent will have to survive without British help till better boats are invented.

UGG!

UGG!

DON'T TALK WITH YOUR MOUTH FULL. I CAN'T UNDERSTAND A WORD YOU'RE SAYING!

HE'S SUCH A SHOW-OFF

1 Dates are very nice in sticky toffee pudding. If you are really hungry then you can cook the dates on this page into a pudding and serve them with custard. This is a book with dates you can eat and not get fat. Yet another Horrible Histories first.

I'D RATHER HAVE A NEANDERTHAL

2800 BC

Brits begin to build Stonehenge in England, while the Irish have built New Grange. Stonehenge is a team effort with stone from Wales being dragged across to make this funny stone circle. No one really knows why they bothered.

2400 BC

People start burying their dead (which is less messy than leaving them in the living room to rot). They place beakers in the graves.

2000 BC

End of the Stone Age as Brits start to use bronze.

1000 BC

Brits are building hill forts. Looks as if they are planning punch-ups with their neighbours. Nothing much will change for the next 3,000 years.

750 BC

The Celts are here. They will end up going west – Ireland, Wales and Scotland are full of them to this day.

390 BC

The Celt cousins in Gaul (France) attack Rome. Big mistake. In 225 BC the Romans strike back and conquer Gaul. The rotten Romans are just across the English Channel – next stop Britain...

We don't know how prehistoric Brits thought. But we can guess what they did from the bits they left behind. And some of the bits are gruesome…

Funeral stew

In Wales there's a stone burial chamber called Barclodiad y Gawres. Archaeologists have worked out that there was a revolting ritual at the funeral of two boys in prehistoric times.

- The bodies were cremated till the flesh burned off.
- The bones were scraped, mixed with sheep bones and buried under a layer of earth inside the chamber.
- Next to the buried body bits a fire was lit under a water pot.
- This stew was stirred into the water…

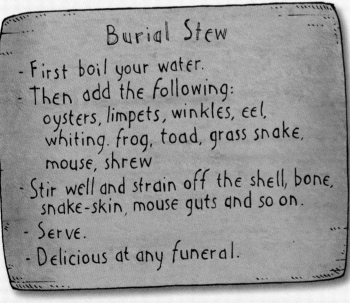

Burial Stew

- First boil your water.
- Then add the following:
  oysters, limpets, winkles, eel, whiting, frog, toad, grass snake, mouse, shrew
- Stir well and strain off the shell, bone, snake-skin, mouse guts and so on.
- Serve.
- Delicious at any funeral.

The rubbish left from the tasty soup was poured onto the dying fire and trampled down to put it out.

They ate mouse? Tasteless but true.

Blood-chilling barrows

Stone Agers were often buried in barrows. (No, dummy, that *doesn't* mean they were stuck in a *wheel*barrow instead of a coffin. 'Barrows' or 'cairns' are what archaeologists call the mounds where humans were buried.)

Barrows were built of earth, cairns of stone. The materials could be heaped over the corpses or there could be a stone or wooden room built and then covered over.

A barrow was just a little house for your putrefying pals. Some archaeologists reckon they were made to look like the Stone Age houses of the living – a sort of retirement hostel for the dead where they would feel at home.

There were different types of barrow and some have been given cute names by archaeologists…

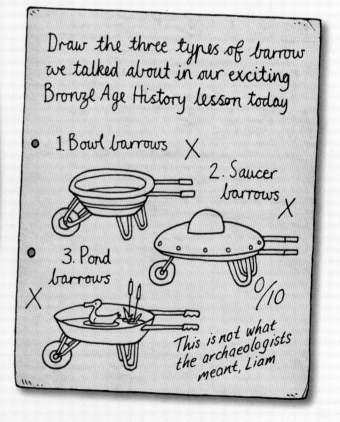

Draw the three types of barrow we talked about in our exciting Bronze Age History lesson today

- 1. Bowl barrows ✗
- 2. Saucer barrows ✗
- 3. Pond barrows ✗

0/10

This is not what the archaeologists meant, Liam

These barrows are found all over the world and were still being used by people like the Vikings up until the Middle Ages. The most common types of barrows built during the earlier Neolithic Age are long barrows. They are called that because, believe it or not, they are *long*!

The mystery of Fussell's Barrow

A good example of a long barrow is the Fussell's Lodge Barrow – an early English barrow.

Archaeologists reckon it took at least ten people to build it. Fussell's Lodge is a log house over 100 metres long. This low wooden house was then buried under a *thousand* tonnes of chalk.

The chalk was dug out of trenches at the side of the lodge using only picks made of deer antlers. Digging must have been back-breaking work and carrying the chalk over to the barrow must have been exhausting…

At one end of a long barrow there was usually a 'mortuary house'. That's where the dead body was left to rot till the flesh fell off, and where the bones were scraped clean before they were buried. The barrows could be re-entered so people could perform rituals with the bones. Fussell's Lodge was used for hundreds of years then abandoned.

Then, in the later Neolithic and Bronze Age, the barrows changed to 'round' barrows. Bet you'll never guess what shape they were! Yes! They were triangular … no, only joking. They were shaped as a round dome – like a giant Christmas pudding that is trying to get in *The Guinness Book of Records*.

Horrible henges

Some bits of Brits' buildings are a mystery to us. Archaeologists can explain how Stonehenge was built in the days before cranes and bulldozers. They've experimented with raising stones using ropes and wood. They can tell you *when* it was built and show how it used to look. But they *can't* agree on what happened inside the stone circle. There have been some strange ideas:

But no Egyptian remains have ever been found there. So let's forget *that* idea.

But Stonehenge was around long before 1600 BC. Forget *that* idea too.

Would you Adam-and-Eve it?[2] That charming idea was put forward in 1943 by a Scotsman who maybe had porridge instead of brains.

Errr … *you* may like to believe that...

Stony circle

There are stone circles all over the British Isles. Many stone-circle legends say the stones were once people or animals. Others say the stones were…

- A complete wedding party, turned to stone for dancing on a Sunday (Stanton Drew, Avon, England)
- Three women who sinned by working on a Sunday (Moelfre Hill, Wales)
- Giants who refused to be christened when Christianity came to the land (Western Isles of Scotland)
- Women who gave false evidence that led to a man being hanged (Cottrell, South Wales)
- A girl running away from a wizard who wanted to marry her (Aberdeen, Scotland)
- A cow, a witch and a fisherman (Inisbofin, Ireland)
- A giant and his seven sons who went to war with a wizard (Kerry, Ireland)
- A mermaid's children (Cruckancornia, Ireland)

Lots of places said the stones were robbers caught stealing from churches, or history teachers who gave impossibly hard homework and were turned to stone by pupils with witch powers … you wish!

2 That's Cockney rhyming slang for 'believe it', okey dokey?

ROTTEN ROMAN BRITAIN

The rotten Romans built a wall across northern England and made Scotland – they made the Scots, Irish and Welsh feel like 'outsiders'. And over the years these outsiders learned to hate the 'insiders' – the English. It led to a lot of Brit blood being spilled.

TERRIBLE TIMELINE

55 BC
Roman Julius Caesar lands. He came, he saw – he went back home to Rome. After all...

54 BC
Caesar's back. But it's too much trouble to conquer the Britons in the south of England. He leaves. After all...

AD 43
Emperor Claudius arrives and conquers the Britons in the south and east of England. This time the rotten Romans want to stay. After all...

AD 60
The Britons in England revolt. They are led by Queen Boudica. She burns down the temple for 'God' Claudius and massacres every helpless Roman she can find. But the Romans win through in the end. Boudica poisons herself (maybe).

AD 80
The Roman governor of Britain, Julius Agricola, invades Scotland. The people there are called Caledonians, so he calls the place ... er ... 'Caledonia', and then massacres up to 10,000 of them.

AD 133

Roman Emperor Hadrian builds a wall all the way across the middle of Britain to keep the Caledonians out of Roman England – two million tons and 140 km of rock and soil to keep out the killer Celts in kilts. (Note: in the 21st century it no longer works.)

AD 137

Romans build a turf and timber wall from the Firth to the Clyde but it's a struggle to keep the Celts out (or in). This is the Antonine wall.

AD 211

The Romans finally give up trying to conquer the Caledonians and stick with Hadrian's wall as their border.

AD 285

And here come the Saxons, Jutes and those Angles who will give the south of Britain its new name – Angle-land (that's England to you and me). At first they are just pirates attacking the south coast.

AD 296

Tribes from France attack Roman London.

AD 367

Tribes from Scotland and Ireland come down from the north as well as Saxon pirates from the east. B-I-G trouble. Worst of all some of the northern attackers, the Attacotti, are said to be cannibals.

AD 408

The Saxon attacks get stronger in the south as the Roman forces rush off home to help defend the city against barbarians.

AD 409

The Romans go home and the Scoti tribe (from Ireland) move in to south-west Scotland and found the kingdom of Dalriada.

Rotten Roman Britain

The first B-I-G invasion of Britain was by the ruthless Romans of Emperor Claudius in AD 43.

Some of the Brits loved being ruled by the Romans and enjoyed Roman ways. They learned Latin and took to togas, they thought baths were brilliant and made beasts of themselves at banquets.

But the Brits who rebelled were vicious in their vengeance. A Roman writer Tacitus wrote about the fighting in AD 58…

The Britons took no prisoners and didn't sell their captives as slaves. They didn't go in for any of the usual trading in war. They wasted no time in getting down to the bloody business of hanging, burning and crucifying. It was as if they were in a hurry to finish their revenge and fill themselves with the blood of their enemies before they could be stopped.

Big bad Boudica

The biggest Brit rebellion was led by Queen Boudica. She rampaged round the country and massacred people in Colchester and St Albans and then slaughtered 70,000 in London. The English Channel was said to be purple with Roman blood. (That would make paddling in the sea at Dover a bit messy.)

At last she came up against the little Roman army of Suetonius Paulinus. She had 250,000 fighters and it looked like a walkover. But the Brits parked their ox-carts with their food and tents and families and set off on a wild charge. The Romans drove them back. The Brits couldn't escape because the ox-carts formed a wall.

Dying Brits fell among dead oxen as they were slaughtered. 80,000 Brits died, only 400 Romans. (At least that's what the Romans said!)

Queen Boudica died of shock – or maybe she poisoned herself. We'll never know for certain.

Now you'd think the Romans would be happy, wouldn't you? But one Roman general, Poenius Postumius, had refused to join the fight against Boudica. He was chicken. After the battle Poenius Postumius was so ashamed. What did he do? Killed himself. Quick clean poison like Boudica?

No. Much messier. He placed a sword to his belly and fell on it.

THEY SAID HE WAS GUTLESS. BUT LOOK – HE HAD LOTS OF THEM

HORRIBLE HISTORIES NOTE:
Don't try this at home. It makes a real mess on the carpet and your parents don't have servants to clear up after you the way the Romans did.

Roman in the gloamin'

Some historians reckon up to 50,000 Romans died trying to conquer Caledonia. But don't feel too sorry for the Romans. Remember – *they* started it! The *Romans* were the invaders.

IF WE DIDN'T INVADE THEY MIGHT HAVE HURT US IN THE FUTURE

OH YEAH, IT'S SO MUCH BETTER THAT THEY HURT US NOW

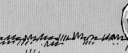

The Romans didn't conquer Caledonia. But they did bring all the Caledonian tribes together. They forgot their squabbles to face the rotten Romans.

At the battle of Mons Graupius in AD 84 the Caledonians lost. The Romans burned Caledonian homes and drove the surviving warriors into the mountains.

That's when the Caledonian leader Calgacus made one of those famous speeches that has gone down in history...

The Romans make a desert and they call it peace.

Great stuff. Pity that line was probably just made up by a Roman writer called Tacitus.[3] In fact some historians say he even made up the Caledonian leader Calgacus!

Then suddenly, two years after winning at Mons Graupius, the Romans packed up and left the Caledonians in peace. (There was trouble over in Romania and they couldn't spare the troops to stay in Scotland.)

Another forty years later Emperor Hadrian built his wall and said, 'Right lads, the Roman Empire stops *here*. Let them have their rotten Caledonia.' (Except Hadrian said it in Latin.)

WHAT DID HADRIAN SAY?

HE SAID THE EMPIRE ENDS HERE

IT'S THE END OF THE EMPIRE!

3 But learn this line anyway and a get better mark in your history tests.

Lindow Lament

The Romans also marched against the Brits in Wales. They thought the Brit priests (Druids) were leading Brit rebellions from their temples in the forests of north Wales.

There's a dead man in the British Museum in London that proves you don't want to mess with dodgy Druids. Well, he's more a *half-dead* man because only half of his body is on show!

In 1984 a mechanical digger was cutting through turf in Lindow, Cheshire when it came across this shrivelled body. Archaeologists and historians were excited by the discovery... They have a very sick idea of excitement, you understand.

They examined the body. The chemicals in the swampy land had preserved him like a pickled onion in vinegar. The one and only ancient Briton face to be seen in modern times!

The historians then set about discovering who he was and how he died ... and it looked like a gruesome story. The man had well-shaped fingernails so he wasn't a peasant. And his death seems to have been some sort of cruel and cut-throat Celtic sacrifice.

Some historians have suggested he could have been a sacrifice to the Gods to help the Celts fight the Romans. Or the Lindow man could have agreed to be sacrificed to help his people. Creepy!

We'll never be sure. But we do know he'd been bashed on the head, strangled, had his throat cut and was thrown into the bog to drown (if he wasn't dead by then).

What would *you* do with Lindow man, who was killed and dumped in a bog?

Would you give him a nice burial and let him rest in peace? Would you put a headstone over his grave with a poem? Probably.

What have the horrible historians done with him? Stuck him in a glass case for people like you and me to gawp at. The *least* they could do was give him an *epitaph* - a message from the dead to the living. Maybe you could write one.

This is just a suggestion. . .

The Lindow Lament,

OR

The Man With No Name Who Wishes He Had One

*The Celts they came and took me in the middle
of the night,
And I knew if they meant business, I was dead.
They never asked permission, said no 'Please,'
or 'By your leave.'
They simply went and bashed me on the head.*
(Twice)

*They used a choking cord until they cut off all
me breath,
They used me like some sacrificial goat.
When they were really sure that I was in the
arms of death,
The rotten bleeders went and cut me throat.*
(Messy)

*So all you living people, see the fate that I
was dealt.
Captured by the cruel and wicked Druids.
Think yourself dead lucky you don't have to
face those Celts,
Who would drain you dry of all your body fluids.*
(Blood)

*They laid me here all shrivelled up - no peace,
no grave, no name;
A wrinkled mummy cut off at the pelvis.
A label calls me 'Lindow Man', and that's my
lasting fame.
I'd rather be a Percy, Joe . . . or Elvis.*
(Wouldn't you?)

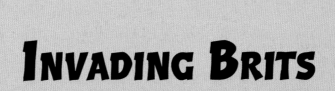

INVADING BRITS

The Romans may have been the first proper invaders of Britain. But they weren't the last. Britain seems to have been the target of half the world – from the French to the Americans.[4] England was often the target of the foreign invaders – and sometimes those invaders had the help of the Irish, Welsh and Scots to get there. Meanwhile, the English invaded all three neighbours time and time again. It seems you just can't trust the people next door.

The year 1066 is supposed to be the most important date in English history. On 14 October that year, William the Conqueror met and beat King Harold of England at the Battle of Hastings. It changed English history for ever.

You don't need reminding of the story of that day.

You do? Oh, very well, but it's so well known you can have just enough to remind you but not the whole lot.

Here it is with some important words missing. Replace the numbers with the correct words.

ENGLAND

LONDON

HASTINGS

the trouble started with king edward the confessor. he was king of england and he promised his throne to william of normandy. he knew harold, head man of england, had his 7 on it and wanted his 9 on it. mind you, harold himself had promised the throne to william. harold went across to normandy and put his hand on a box of 1 from saint rasyphus and...

4 Yes. There HAS been an American-led invasion of Britain and you will find out when. But not many people remember that. You will know it if you read on. Then you can go off and boast about it.

...saint ravennus. harold said, 'the throne is all yours, william.'

but edward died at the end of 1065 and harold grabbed his throne.

william was furious. and the pope was on william's side. 'go and invade england with my blessing. and here is a ring with the 2 of saint peter for luck.'

william started to build ships and build an army to attack. but, before he could, harold faced another invader. the viking harald hardrada – and, as you know, hardrada means tough-talking.

hardrada was one of those vikings who got himself into a wild state before a battle and fought like an animal – the vikings called them 'berserkers'. he had long 2 and a thick 3.

harold hurried to stamford bridge in yorkshire to meet hardrada in battle. it was hardrada who ended up with an axe in the 4. one of his berserker friends held the bridge till an english soldier floated under it and stuck a spear up his 9.

meanwhile william had landed at hastings. he jumped from the ship and looked a bit of a plonker when he fell forward up to his 5 in water. (that must have washed the 2 of st peter in the ring.) but crafty william grabbed handful of sand, turned to his men and said, 'see how i've seized english land already?'

on 13th october 1066 harold arrived and the battle began the next day. harold sat on a hilltop and watched the normans struggle to get up on tired 6. william wore the 1 of saint rasyphus and saint ravennus around his neck for luck. but every 10 seemed to fall short. so william ordered the archers to fire higher and one struck harold in the 7. the normans rushed forward and hacked wounded harold to the ground. they stripped him and cut off his 6 and 5 finally they lopped off his head with a chop to the 4.

the battle was over and william was the one to get his 9 in the english throne.

Clues? You don't need clues? Oh, very well there are 10 missing words – head, legs, beard, bones, arrow, bum, arms, neck, hair, eye

Answers: 1 = bones, 2 = hair, 3 = beard, 4 = neck, 5 = arms, 6 = legs, 7 = eye, 8 = head, 9 = bum, 10 = arrow

In fact, when Harold was hacked to pieces one of William's knights cut off Harold's naughty bits. William was furious and sent the knight back to Normandy in disgrace. 'You don't treat a noble enemy like that, *mon ami,*' William said.

Mum's army

Everybody remembers the first invasion from France, in 1066 – they remember King Harold the hero who died with an arrow in his eye. But he was a *man* and a king so he's remembered even though he lost.

Sadly Jemima Nicholas and the Pembroke Mum's army have been almost forgotten. She was a woman, of course, and it doesn't seem to matter that she faced another French invasion and she actually won! (You may have been reading this in French if she hadn't!)

Here are ten famous facts about her dramatic – and almost forgotten – story.

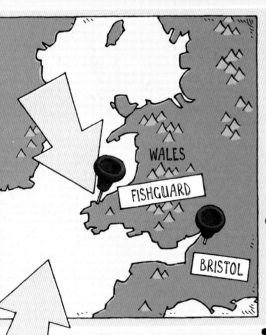

1 On 22 February 1797, 1,500 French troops known as the Black Legion, landed at Carreg Wastad, near Fishguard, on the west coast of Wales. The main French force was planning to invade Ireland and set it free from British rule.

2 The French sent these 1,500 men to attack Bristol – a sort of diversion from the main attack. But gales blew them past Bristol so they sailed round to Fishguard.

3 The French expected the Welsh to rise up and fight with them against the English! Bad idea. But they picked a good place to land. The defenders only had eight cannon in the whole of Fishguard – and those cannon only had three cannonballs! So what did the defenders do? They fired blanks! It kept the French quiet for hours till Lord Cawdor arrived with a proper army.

4 The French found some barrels of wine that had been washed ashore the week before and they drank it all. There's a story that one Frenchman fell asleep in a farmhouse. He was so drunk he woke in the night and heard the click of a musket and fired at his enemy. It turned out to be the tick of a grandfather clock.

5 The local POSH people grabbed their money and ran away. But the peasants grabbed pitchforks, scythes and even spades and joined Lord Cawdor's army.

6 Jemima Nicholas – a local cobbler – went out into her fields that day and saw a dozen French soldiers wandering around. They were poor soldiers – half of the French army were criminals fresh out of jail. Some of them still had ankle irons on. They were starving and drunk. Jemima caught them chasing her sheep and chickens to eat.

7 She picked up a pitchfork and pointed it at them at them. They threw down their weapons. Jemima marched them down to the local lock-up. She became a Welsh heroine and was awarded a pension of £50 a year for life.

8 Jemima and her friends joined Lord Cawdor's army to attack the rest of the French on the beach – just to see the sport really. They caught one or two French on the way. One was bashed over the head with a chair leg, another was thrown down a well.

9 The French on the beach saw the women's red cloaks in the distance. They thought they were more redcoat soldiers coming to attack, so they threw down their weapons.

10 But the French army was led by an old American, Colonel Tate. The last invasion of Britain was American-led. Not a lot of people know that.

After this defeat the French never tried invading Britain again. In fact no one has landed on Britain's shores since. (Unless you count a few German pilots shot down in the Second World War.)

Cut-throat Cromwell

One invasion was so cruel it is still remembered today. It was the invasion of Ireland by England's Oliver Cromwell in 1649.

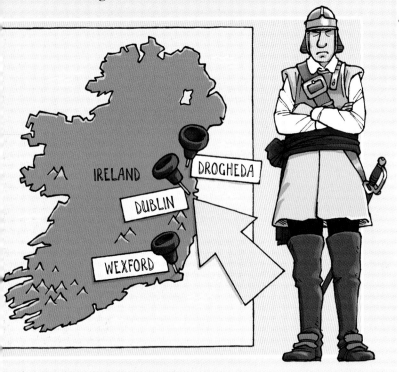

Oliver Cromwell, Protector of England, had cut off King Charles I's head and wasn't going to be too bothered about having a few thousand Irish rebels massacred.

His visit is still remembered in Ireland as 'Mallacht Cromail' – the curse of Cromwell. What did Cromwell do that was so bad? It's hard to pick the worst, but here are a few examples with marks out of ten.

WE'RE USING THE ALL-NEW CROMAILOMETER SCORING SYSTEM – FROM 'ONE' – PRETTY BAD, TO 'TEN' – UNFORGIVABLY MONSTROUS

1 Cromwell was strict with his own troops and had two hanged for stealing hens from an Irish peasant woman.

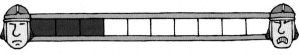

2 At Drogheda (north of Dublin) the defenders of a church locked themselves in the steeple. Cromwell's soldiers dragged seats from the church and burned them under the steeple to roast the defenders alive. (One defender jumped and suffered only a broken leg. The English admired his courage and let him live!)

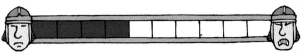

3 Cromwell said of Drogheda, 'I ordered my men not to spare anyone who was carrying a weapon.' This was a usual way of fighting. Cromwell would have said he wasn't to blame when his men supposedly killed women, children and priests.

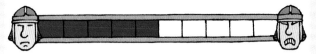

4 Sir Arthur Aston, English Catholic leader of Drogheda's defence, was captured. His wooden leg was ripped off and he was beaten to death with it. Soldiers believed it was full of gold – all they got were splinters.

5 Priests in Wexford were flogged to death then their bodies were flung into drains. Soldiers often dressed in Catholic priests' clothes to make fun of their victims, though it was said that they sickened and died soon after!

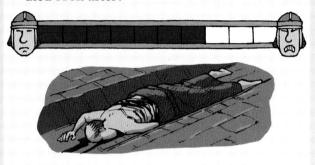

6 Cromwell himself led the charge on Mill Mount Tower in Drogheda. The defenders surrendered and expected to be spared. Of course they were all killed.

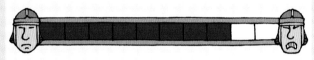

7 In Wexford 200 women and children were herded into the marketplace to be slaughtered. Cromwell explained this was a 'righteous judgement' from God … so that's all right.

8 It was said that when they attacked some well-defended places the English soldiers took Irish babies and held them in front as shields.

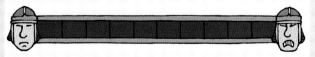

There were spooky stories that lived on after Cromwell had gone. They told of…

- An executioner who killed a priest and was splashed with his blood. The blood could never be washed out of the man's clothing.

- A very holy monk who pulled up the hood of his habit and the English bullets bounced off it.

Ireland hated Cromwell – and Cromwell hated Ireland. He was seasick when he crossed the Irish sea and never felt well all the time he was there. Maybe that's what made him so vicious.

DREADFUL DARK-AGE BRITAIN

The Dark Ages weren't dark. I mean, it wasn't 24 hours of night-time every day. We are just a bit 'in the dark' about them. The Brits were too busy living their lives to write boring old history books about them. And some of the history books they did write were a bit dodgy – legends and lies mixed in with the truth.

TERRIBLE TIMELINE

AD 432

Saint Patrick arrives in Ireland from Britain and single-handedly converts Ireland to Christianity (they say). He can't have stopped to sleep or eat if that's true! But he certainly stopped in 461, when he dropped down dead.

AD 450-ish

The most powerful Brit leader is Vortigern. He invites the Angle tribe leaders Hengist and Horsa over from Germany to help fight the Saxons. Big mistake. Hengist and Horsa's Germans decide to stay.

AD 500-ish

According to legend, King Arthur leads the Celtic Britons in a fight against the Angles and Saxons. But in 539 he is killed by his own nephew, Mordred. Some say he is from Wales.

HA! I COULD CONVERT THIS LOT WITH ONE HAND TIED BEHIND MY BACK

? ? ?

HE'S STOPPED CONVERTING

AND BREATHING

HI, WE'RE HENGIST AND HORSA AND WE'RE HERE TO HELP

HI, WE'RE HERE TO PUT UP SOME HOUSES, HAVE SOME KIDS AND SETTLE DOWN

KING ARTHUR'S OWN FLESH AND BLOOD

KING ARTHUR'S FLESH AND BLOOD

SOMEHOW I THOUGHT CAMELOT WOULD BE BIGGER

Barmy Brits believe Arthur's sleeping and he'll be back when Britain is in danger.

615

At the Battle of Chester the English King Aethelfrith beats the Welsh King Selyf. 1500 monks prayed for the Welsh to win – so Aethelfrith has them massacred too. The Welsh are cut off from their friends in England and Scotland. The monks are just cut off from their heads, arms, legs...

672

Ecgfrith of Northumbria massacres a Pict army and a lot of its leaders. They were invading northern England so it served them right. But he'll pay for it. Because in 685 Ecgfrith tries to invade Pictland to teach the Pict raiders a lesson. The Picts massacre him and his army at Nechtan Pass. Some lesson.

TROUBLE CLOCK

YOU PRAYED FOR YOUR SELYF, WITH A SELYF-SERVING SELYF-INTEREST SHOWING NOTHING BUT A SELYF-CENTRED SELYF REGARD. NOW YOU ONLY HAVE YOUR SELYF TO BLAME FOR YOUR SELYF-DESTRUCTIVE SELYF SACRIFICE

I'M SO ASHAMED OF MYSELYF

SHREDDED PICTS WITH ECG ON TOP

BEATEN ECG

718

War between two great Irish monasteries - Clonmacnois and Durrow - in which 200 are killed. Monks mash monks! So much for men of peace - more like men in pieces.

793

The Vikings arrive in northern England. They massacre, rob and soon they'll settle too. By 840 they've set up the new city of Dublin in Ireland.

798

The Saxons aren't too bothered by the odd Viking raid ... yet. So they go on fighting each other. King Ceowulf of Mercia (the Midlands) attacks King Edbert of Kent. Ed is captured and Ceowulf has the Kent king's eyes put out and his hands cut off.

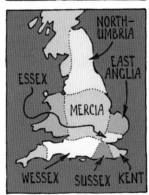

806

The Vikings go round to Iona in Scotland and massacre the monks there. Where's Arthur when you need him? Still sleeping?

878

Alfred the Great of Wessex fights back and says, 'You Vikings keep the north and east - you can even call it Danelaw. My Saxons will keep the south and west - Wessex.' And they had a deal.

1014

Blood rains from the sky, soldiers are attacked by spears that fly out of walls and by ravens with iron beaks. (That's what horrible historians of the time say.) In an Irish v. Viking battle at Clontarf the Irish King Brian Boruma wins ... but is killed before he can be king of all Ireland.

1018

In the Battle of Carham the northern English are defeated and the winner, King Malcolm II becomes king of their land too. Later, it would be part of Scotland.

1066

The Normans arrive and still Arthur doesn't show. That must be one deep sleep.

Killing King Ken II

Some of the terrible tales from the Dark Ages are a bit fantastic, so it may be better to tell them as fairy tales – in fact, if you have a nasty little brother you may like to tell him this as a bedside story so he has nightmares.

Once upon a time there was a beautiful queen and her name was Queen Finella.

Finella was lovely, but she was ever so sad because her dear son Malcolm had died. She cried and cried, but that did no good. So, in the end, she decided to find out how Malcolm had died. They say she was a little bit of a witch, but a good witch.

Finella went to her cauldron and stirred the magic brew, chanting:

Eye of bat and a sprinkle of talcum;
Tell me who killed poor little Malcolm!

The pot bubbled and boiled and then it answered:

Your Malcolm died, the poor young thing,
Murdered by a rotten king!
Dry your eyes, good sweet Finella,
Old King Ken's the guilty fella.

Now the only King Ken that Queen Fin kenned (knew) was cruel King Kenneth in Kincardine, the kingdom next door.
Finella knew she wasn't strong enough to raise an army and go

to war with King Kenneth. So she came up with a clever plan instead.

She used all her magic arts to make a brass statue of King Kenneth. It was yellow as Finella's curls and as shiny as the sun on the loch. In the glistening statue's hand there was an apple covered in a rainbow of jewels. When the statue was finished, she put it in the middle of her finest room in Fettercairn and invited King Kenneth to come and see it.

Kenneth arrived and Finella gave a low curtsey. 'I am your humble servant, King Ken,' she said. 'Please accept this gift.'

Cruel Ken looked at the statue and said, 'I'll never get that thing home on horseback!'

Finella smiled sweetly and said, 'Just the apple, Ken. Reach out and take the apple.'

The killing king stretched out a hand while Finella ducked. As soon as his hand touched the apple a dozen hidden crossbows in the walls fired poison arrows into his body.

'It was all a trick!' Ken cried as he died.

'And it serves you jolly well, right,' Finella said with her sweet smile.

And Queen Finella lived happily ever after until she died an even more horrible death than Kenneth.

The End.

Verse and worse

In England, the Saxons had no television. (Even if they had then it would have been useless because they had no electricity to switch it on.) So they entertained themselves with long stories to pass the long winter nights. Now a storyteller can remember a story better if the tale is turned into a poem. Even bits of their history books were written in poetry when the writer got excited about it!

In 937, when King Athelstan defeated an army of invading Irish with their savage Scots friends, the Saxons' success was recorded in the *Anglo Saxon Chronicle*. This would be one of the good bits – the good but gruesome bits you like to hear in your favourite fairy tales – you know the sort of thing: 'Ooooh Grandmama! What big eyes you have!' 'All the better to smell you with.'

Imagine those savage Saxons sitting round the fire and listening to this part…

The field grew dark with the soldiers' blood
And the corpses were left behind.
The bodies they left to be shared by the beasts
Like the ravens in dusty black coats.
And the grey-coated eagle, the greedy war hawk,
The great grey-haired beast of the forest.

You could try reciting that to someone you don't like, just as they are about to tuck in to their school dinner!

Heledd's savage song

The Saxons, like the Romans before them and the Normans after them, attacked the Welsh. The Welsh wrote poems to remember their dead heroes … even losers like Cynddylan. This bloodthirsty poem was said to be written by dead Cynddylan's sister, Heledd. In English it may sound a bit like this…

The Song of Heledd

My brothers were killed at a single stroke
Defending the poor town of Tern.
The blood on the fields was as common as grass
And the hall of Cynddylan is burned.

Cynddylan would ride into battle and kill.
His heart was as wild as a boar,
The enemy corpses were two layers deep
When my brother he rode out to war.

Cynddylan he rode in a fine purple cloak
And he treated his guests like a lord.
Now his white flesh it lies in a coffin of black
His life claimed by the vile Saxon hordes.

Cynddylan will never return to his hall
It is dark, there's no fire and no bed.
I lie sick and feeble, and stroke the dark hair
That will never grow grey on his head.

Cheerful stuff, eh?

NASTY NORMAN BRITAIN

William the Conqueror arrived in 1066 and conquered the English. His knights then moved on to Wales and Ireland. Scotland was told to behave itself or the nasty Normans would go and sort them out too. Yet again the rulers of Britain lived in England and the other three learned to loathe the big brother.

TERRIBLE TIMELINE

1070

Vicious King Malcolm III of Scotland meets Saxon Princess Margaret when a storm drives their ships into Wearmouth in Durham. She changes the Scottish church from loosely Christian to strict Roman Catholic.

1071

William the Conqueror invades Scotland and makes Malcolm and Scotland his subjects. This doesn't stop Malcolm raiding England when he feels like it.

1120

Norman King Henry I loses his only two sons, William and Richard. Very careless. His sons were on 'The White Ship' crossing to France. The crew of the ship were probably drunk. They certainly ended in the drink. Henry has no male heirs now. This will cause trouble when he dies and people start scrapping for the throne!

1135

Henry I has chosen nephew Stephen to be the next king. Henry's daughter, Empress Matilda says, 'I'll fight you for the crown!' The wars bring almost 20 years of misery to England. These times are known as 'The Anarchy'.

As usual, when the English start fighting each other, someone tries to invade them. This time it's the sneaky Scots in 1138. The Scots are defeated.

1153

The war ends when Stephen agrees that Matilda's son can have the throne when he dies. A year later Stephen keeps his promise - and dies. Peace at last.

1154

Henry II of England is from Anjou - an area in France to the south of Normandy. The Norman lords in England are no longer calling themselves Normans, but 'English'.

1169

Irish King Dermot loses his throne and, being a bad loser, he invites Normans across to help him try to get it back. They help themselves and almost take over Ireland.

1170

Dublin is captured by Norman-English armies and won't be free of English control again till 1922. (That's 752 years if you have a calculator handy. Or a long, long time if you haven't).

1173

King William, the Lion of Scotland, is caught by English knights when he gets lost in a fog near Alnwick. He has to promise to obey the English king. Breaking this promise by invading again will lead to hundreds of years of horrors.

Caught red-handed

Bishop Odo of Bayeux was William the Conqueror's half-brother. In conquered England he acted as a judge and, with the help of a jury, he decided arguments.

Being a member of a jury today means you have to be fair and honest. If you're not then you could go to prison. But prison isn't as bad as the punishment Odo saved for cheating jurymen in his day.

If there had been newspapers in Norman times then the case may have been reported like this…

THE Norman News **1066** THE TAPESTRY

ENGLISH EDITION

PRICE 2 EGGS

free family ticket

POSH NOSH! MAKE KING WILLIAM'S FEUDAL NOODLES! P27-36

'THRILLS and KILLS' ★★★★★ says our embroidery reviewer

EXCLUSIVE

JURY FURY

Bishop Odo gave the punishers some punishment today … and it didn't half hurt! Twelve members of the jury in the Islesham Manor Case have been found guilty of lying in court. Our readers will remember the case where the Bishop of Rochester and the Sheriff of Cambridge were arguing over who owned the stately home. The twelve good men and untrue of the jury decided to give it to the Sheriff.

That might have been an end to it but a Rochester monk made a sensational claim. The jury had not played fair, and, what's more, the mean monk could prove it!

Today Bishop Odo (the Basher Bishop, or Bish Bash as our readers know him) heard the evidence and decided the jury were indeed as bent as a nine-groat piece. First Bish Bash fined them till their purses were empty as Harold's eye-socket. Then he ordered that the guilty men should have their right hands plunged into boiling water.

Our ace reporter, Hugh Je Scoop, watched the sentence being carried out. 'I'd like to get my hand on the monk that fingered me,' muttered one victim (who wishes to remain nameless). His wife Jeanne de Yorke (who also wishes to remain nameless) said, 'I told him that trying his hand at lying to Odo would get him in hot water. Once Odo takes matters in hand he always wins hands down. You have to hand it to him. Wasn't I right?'

Little villeins

The Normans ran their countries under a 'feudal system'. Imagine that as a pyramid...

This is the king who sits at the top and owns the lot.

> THAT'S WHY THEY CALL ME 'YOUR HIGHNESS'. 'COZ I'M UP HIGH, SEE

These are the barons who guard the king's land, and train the men to fight for the king who sits at the top and owns the lot.

> BLIMEY, IT'S A LONG WAY UP. SHOULDN'T THERE BE A HANDRAIL OR SOMETHING?

These are the knights who look after the villages, and fight for their barons who guard the king's land, and train the men to fight for the king who sits at the top and owns the lot.

> NICE VIEW

> IF YOU LIKE EGYPTIAN DESERTS

These are the villeins and serfs who work on the land and work for the knights who look after the villages, who fight for their barons who guard the king's land, and train the men to fight for the king who sits at the top and owns the lot.

> AT LEAST WE HAVEN'T GOT AS FAR TO FALL

> OI! HOP IT YOU LOT. WE DIDN'T BUILD THESE THINGS FOR YOU TO CLAMBER ALL OVER! GO FIND SOMETHING ELSE FOR YOUR FEUDAL EXPLANATIONS

And lowest of all were the village children – nothing much changes there, then.

Was it pleasant being a peasant child? You'd have no school to go to! (So you couldn't learn to read and have the joy of *Horrible Histories* books, of course.)

31

The Normans are coming

William the Conqueror conquered England in 1066 but it was another 100 years before the nasty Normans got around to battering the Irish.

'Strongbow' was the nickname of the Norman Richard, Earl of Pembroke. King Dermott MacMurrough of Leinster invited Strongbow to come to Ireland to sort out his old enemy Rory O'Connor. Naturally Strongbow ended up taking over a large part of Ireland. Never trust a Norman! (The battered Irish believed that King Dermott rotted to death as a punishment for the great sin of bringing over the Normans.)

In 1170 Strongbow's army landed in Waterford. They decided to terrorise the people into giving in. So they didn't simply execute 70 Waterford leaders … they chopped off their arms, legs and heads and threw the bits off a cliff. Nasty. But not as nasty as the story of Strongbow's son…

And you thought your dad was mean with your pocket money! At least when he threatens you with a 'cut' he doesn't do it with a sword!

scrambled sayings

the irish, scots and welsh all have their own languages. but most people in britain speak english most of the time.

they use the english language to say some pretty potty things – and some curiously clever things if you think about them.

take the irish in the middle ages. they had some puzzling sayings, like 'it's a bad hen that won't scratch herself' meaning people should be able to do their own work. that's useful when your mother tells you to go to the shop or do the washing up. (but not when your pocket money depends on it.)

now you've got the idea, you should have no trouble putting the two halves of these irish proverbs back together. match the first column with the last. (work out what they mean – or simply go around saying them, and everyone will think you're brilliant!)

1 a woman's tongue	a) speaks the truth
2 death	b) is difficult to choose
3 the mouth of the grave	c) is better than a salmon in the sea
4 a trout in the pot	d) can lose his hat in a fairy wind
5 even a tin knocker	e) does not rust
6 between two blind goats it	f) is the poor man's doctor
7 any man	g) will shine on a dirty door
8 when the tongue slips it	h) gives to the needy one

SPORTY BRITS

The British people spent hundreds of years fighting each other. When they didn't have wars to enjoy then they had to beat and batter each other on the sports fields. Here are some of the great and grim games they've played through the ages.

HURLEY HURLEY HURLEY

The Irish have a rough form of hockey known to the Celts as 'hurley' and modern Irish as 'hurling'.

you'll need:

- two teams of 15 players, each with a hurling stick – like a hockey stick with a broad end
- two goals (like five-a-side soccer goals with extended uprights to make an 'H' shape)
- a hard ball like a rounders ball

to play:

1 The aim is to score a 'Goal' – three points if it goes under the crossbar, one point over the crossbar but between the posts.

2 Play like hockey – except you can carry the ball on the hurling stick for as far as you want and you can catch the ball in the hand, but...

3 You can't pick up the ball from the ground in the hand, throw the ball or run with it in the hand for more than two strides.

4 Horrible hurling: you are not allowed to use your stick to batter or trip an opponent ... but ancient warriors are said to have played this game with the head of an enemy.

WARNING

ANY PLAYER TRYING TO PLAY WITH A HEAD TODAY WILL BE BANNED FOR ONE GAME – AND PROBABLY LOCKED UP FOR LIFE. REFEREES DO NOT ACCEPT THE EXCUSE, 'BUT THE CUT-THROAT CELTS DID IT'.

Scotland has its own national sports. Here are some other peculiar pastimes they have tried through the ages...

Hurley hacket

(or summer sledging)

to play:

1 Take a dead horse (plenty of those around in the Middle Ages) and boil its head till the flesh drops off.

2 Take the clean skull to Heading Hill in Stirling. (It's really Be-heading Hill because that was the place where they gave chops to tops.)

3 Use the skull as a sledge and slide down the hill.

If you can't get to Stirling then try Calton Hill in Edinburgh, where young people also enjoyed this sport.

If you haven't got a dead horse (or 'hack') then you can't play hurley hacket. But you can play hurley haaky if you have a haaky – a cow.

WARNING
IF YOU REALLY MUST TRY THIS SPORT, THEN WATCH THE COW'S STEER. DON'T GIVE YOU THE CHANCE OF IT JOINT OF MAD COW DISEASE.

WAS YOUR COW MAD WHEN IT DIED?

WELL, IT WASN'T VERY PLEASED*

* WE APOLOGIZE FOR THE USE OF THIS JOKE (AGAIN)

✖ DID YOU KNOW...? ✖

The champion at hurley hacket was King James V who preferred this sort of sledging to ruling the country.

TWISTING THE COW

At the Invergarry Games of 1820 the events included 'dancing, piping, lifting a heavy stone, throwing the hammer and running from the island to Invergarry and back' (six miles). But the strangest event was 'Twisting the legs off a cow'.

you need:
Dead cows – one for each competitor.

to play:
1 Twist off all four legs of the cow
2 The person who does it in the shortest time is the winner.

the prize:
One fat sheep.

At Invergarry at least one man succeeded and won the sheep, but it took him about an hour.

One of the most famous Scottish games is...

Tossing the caber

you need:
A caber - that's a tree trunk without its branches. (Use a telegraph pole if you haven't got a handy tree.)
Lots of room

to play:
1 Pick up the tree trunk and cradle one end in your hands.

2 Throw the caber as far as you can.

3 The caber must hit the ground with the end you are not holding and tilt forward.

to cheat:
If you aren't strong enough to pick up a caber then you could try tossing the pencil. Real weeds can try tossing the matchstick.

Hunt the human

This sport was popular with the Earl of Buchan (1380 – 1424).

to play:
1 Set fire to Rothiemurchus Forest. The fire will drive out any deer, wolves, wild boar and outlaws that live in the forest.
2 Have well-armed hunters waiting outside the forest.
3 Kill everything that flees from the fire.
4 Eat the deer and boar. Leave the dead outlaws for the wolves to eat.

HEN-HUNTING

In 1764 a bored lord in Huntingdon invented a game called 'hunting the hen'. The players had their hands muffled in thick bandages. They had to catch a hen and pull a feather out. The first to take a feather won the hen.

HAPPY HUNTINGDON HEN-HUNTING HERO

HORRIBLE HUNTING

Spain is famous for bull-fighting. Britain has always been famous for hunting animals with hounds.

The deer-hunting of earlier times went out of fashion and fox-hunting became the most popular entertainment for the upper classes. Hare-hunting was popular too because hares didn't run so far.[5] In 1790 a hare actually escaped from the pack and the *Newcastle Chronicle* reported...

The hare fled and, with a wonderful leap, darted through a pane of glass in a window of The Globe Inn. It landed amongst a pile of legal papers since the inn was crowded with lawyers at the time. As soon as they recovered from the shock, the lawyers presented the poor hare to the cook...

You'd think the lawyers would have given it a fair hare trial, wouldn't you? But that's life. Hare today, gone tomorrow.

5 Popular with ladies and gentlemen, that is. Two boys who killed a hare for food were given a public whipping in Reading in 1773.

MEASLY MIDDLE-AGE BRITAIN

It seems everyone was fighting everyone in Britain. When one of the countries got tired of fighting another they just went home and fought themselves. The 'Wars of the Roses' had the English smashing one another till it all came to a bloody end at Bosworth Field.

TERRIBLE TIMELINE

1215

King John upsets everyone in sight – the barons, the Pope, the people. In the end they force him to sign the Great Charter ('Magna Carta' in Latin). It gives some power to the people. John then says, 'I may have signed it but I am going to ignore it!'. And the squabbling is about to break out all over again. John, very kindly, dies. (Or was he poisoned?)

1272

Edward I becomes king and sets about turning England into 'Britain'. He batters the Welsh and he hammers the Scots. This all costs a lot of money which means a lot of taxes for the English peasants.

They are not happy. In fact it won't be too long before they are revolting!

1286

Scottish King Alexander III falls off a cliff and dies. Then the infant Queen Margaret dies and 13 people claim the Scottish throne. One of them is Edward I of England. And he has an army to back him up. Big man, big trouble.

1297

William Wallace leads a rebellion to throw the English out of Scotland. He loses and is executed in 1305. Sad story but it will make an exciting film called Braveheart in 700 years' time – even though it's an American film made in Ireland starring an Australian as Willy Wally.

1306

Robert Bruce takes over the fight against the English. He wins a lot of battles, especially ... 1314, the Battle of Bannockburn. Edward II of England is smashed.

1315–18

Invasion of Ireland by Edward Bruce and Robert Bruce from Scotland. They think the Irish should join the Scots (and Welsh) to bash the English. They fail, but Scots will be up to their sporrans in Northern-Irish life for the rest of history.

1320

Declaration of Arbroath by Scottish earls and barons says, 'It is freedom alone that we fight for.' They also warn Robert the Bruce they'll throw him out if he ever accepts English rule. Tough talk.

1328

Edward III of England agrees to let Scotland be free of English rule. Robert the Bruce rules, OK? Er, no. Not OK. Robert dies and 5-year-old David II takes over for 42 years – when he's not fleeing to France (1333–41) or defeated and imprisoned by the English (1346–57).

1337

Edward III says 'I'm King of France.' Philip VI of France says, 'Oh, no you're not.' Ed invades France, which makes a nice change. And starts a war that will last 116 years. With the help of Welsh archers, the English army win amazing battles. But the war will cost a lot of poor peasant taxes. They won't like that.

1348

The "Black Death" plague arrives in England and will kill a third of the British people – but mainly the poor. If you get huge purple blisters and start spitting blood then it's bad news. But the English in Ireland complain it is killing more of them than it is killing Irish!

THAT'S SO UNFAIR

IS HE SPITTING BLOOD?

NO. HE'S JUST SPITTING

THE SLIMY STUARTS START HERE

1371

Robert II takes the Scottish crown. He is the first of the famous Stuart kings and a weak old man. A writer says 'There were horrible destructions, burnings and slaughters throughout the kingdom.' Nothing unusual, then.

HO-HUM ANOTHER KING, ANOTHER DAY OF MISERY AND MURDER

1381

The English Peasants' Revolt. A 'Poll' Tax causes the trouble. (I said they wouldn't like it.) It's a tax on every 'head' or 'poll' – and as most people have heads most people have to pay it.

...SO IF I CUT MY HEAD OFF I WON'T HAVE TO PAY?

Led by Wat Tyler the peasants march on London to see the king, lopping off a few lordly heads along the way.

1399

Henry IV takes the throne from Richard II. The English are fighting among themselves again. These scraps will be known as 'The Wars of the Roses'. Remember they're still trying to fight the Hundred Years War that began in 1337.

1400s

The English turn the area around Dublin into a sort of fortress called the 'Pale'. The Irish, 'beyond the Pale' were called 'the wild Irish, our enemies' by King Richard II. Just being a 'wild Irish' in England could get you thrown in jail. The English inside the Pale are urged to exterminate the 'wild Irish' outside 'like nettles'. Nice.

1400

Prophets in Wales say that the world is coming to an end in the year 1400.

POLLS ON POLES!

AH-HA!

OOPS! NEARLY FORGOT! I'VE LEFT THE OTHER WAR ON

I'M NOT WILD – JUST A TAD UNKEMPT

I'VE BEEN HACKING BACK THE IRISH ALL DAY – I'M POOPED!

YOU POOR THING, DID YOU GET STUNG MUCH?

I WOULDN'T MAKE ANY PLANS IF I WERE YOU

HOP

ZING

NIBBLE

I DON FEEL WEL

Peasants want to make the most of the time they have left; they booze and fight. They elect Owain Glyndwr as their leader. But by 1415 Glyndwr is beaten and disappears – Wales is left in a right mess.

1406

James I of Scotland is captured by English and held prisoner for 17 years.

1411

One of Scotland's bloodiest battles is fought at Harlaw. But it's Highland Scots attacking Lowland Scots. The Lowlanders win.

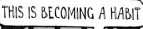

1485

The Battle of Bosworth. King Richard III loses the last big battle of the Wars of the Roses and it's the end of those Normans and Plantagenets. It's a Welsh family, the Tudors, who will take over for the next hundred years or so. Henry VII vows to tame the 'Irish savages'. Not a good start to the Tudor age. Terrible Tudors.

Hammer Ed

The trouble with the Scottish wars in the Middle Ages was that they weren't played by the usual rules.

Scotland was left with a choice of 13 possible kings in 1286 when Alexander III died. The Scots made the mistake of asking King Edward I of England to judge who should get the crown. Edward chose John Balliol, an English Baron, for the Scottish throne. Surprise, surprise!

Then, after four years, Balliol got a bit big for his boots and refused to do what Edward told him. So Edward marched up to Scotland with an army to show Balliol who was boss.

Edward became known as the 'Hammer of the Scots' for his actions. Big Ed started with the border town of Berwick. Forget the rules. He...

- burned the town.
- killed the men, the women and the children.
- ordered that the bodies should be left in the streets so the stench would remind the Scots of his power.

When Ed caught up with John Balliol in church he snatched the crown off the Scottish king's head and threw it to the soldiers to play with. Ed announced that he would take the throne of Scotland for himself.

The Scottish chiefs, bishops and lords were all ordered to go to smelly Berwick to sign a document and say they agreed. The document was known as 'The Ragman's Roll' – a 'ragman', like a miserable Scottish lord of the time, being a beggar.

Scotland was at an all-time low. And then along came William Wallace to lead them against Ed's evil English.

A HUNDRED WAYS WITH HAGGIS

MMM YUMMY!

the **Flying Scotsperson**

5 groats

11 September 1297

WALLACE WALLOPS ENGLISH

BROKEN BRIDGE NOBBLES KNIGHTS

FEAR THE SPEAR says plucky scot Ken MacKilt

William Wallace scored a shock victory over the arrogant English knights. The English crossed the little wooden bridge to where the Scots waited on the slopes of Abbey Craig. But there was no way back when the bridge collapsed. That was the sign for the gallant Scottish spear-men to rush down the hill and strike the mighty knights from their saddles. Scottish spears and Scottish hearts overcame the power of the English swords and battle-axes.

Wallace has been named 'Guardian of Scotland'. If Edward has any sense he'll stay out of our glorious country for good.

Of course it was too good to last. Within a year, Edward I personally led an army to sort out the rebellious Scots. William Wallace told his men, 'I have led you into the ring, now see if you can dance.' But the only dance they were going to do was the dance of death. Wallace's army was shattered and he fled.

Wallace was betrayed and executed in 1304, but Edward died in 1307 and Wallace's friend, Robert Bruce, had the chance to battle against the English.

THE BANNOCK BUGLE

2 groats

LATE KNIGHT EXTRA

24 June 1314

ROBERT ROUTS RAIDERS

BRUCE BATTERS BOHUN

It was the match of the century at Bannockburn today when 7,000 Scots faced a mighty English army of over 20,000 — and won a famous victory. King Robert set the tone with a smashing success in single combat. As he rode at the head of his troops the big-headed English knight, de Bohun, charged him with his lance. The crafty king ducked and as the knight rode past, Robert split the English skull with his axe. 'That was my best axe and I snapped the handle!' Rob roared. That was all the encouragement our brave lads needed to savage the southerners.

Every Scot on the battlefield was a hero today. The English chargers died on the pikes of the Scottish foot-soldiers. A witness says that 'blood lay in pools on the ground'. Victory was Scotland's when English Edward II turned and ran away and his cowardly crew ran after him. They left a fortune in loot for the super Scottish slayers.

Fighting females

The men of England, Ireland, Scotland and Wales were supposed to be full of fighting spirit. But the warrior women had to be just as tough. In Scottish history there are thousands of fighting females who deserve to be remembered.

Black Agnes

The Countess of Dunbar held Dunbar Castle against the English attackers for 19 weeks in 1338. The English smashed her walls with huge catapults. Agnes walked along the top of the castle wall and looked at the scarred walls. Just to annoy the English she dusted the scars with a white handkerchief! Then the English attacked with battering rams. Agnes ordered that the broken walls should be thrown down on top of the batterers. The English gave up and went home.

FLICK FLICK

Kate Douglas

When assassins came to murder James I his door should have been barred with a beam of wood held in two sockets. Then the only way to break in would have been to charge till they shattered the beam. But the beam had been stolen by plotters inside the house. To give James a chance to escape, the queen's waiting-woman, Kate Douglas, jammed her arm in the sockets. Now the only way for the attackers to get in the room was to charge till they shattered her arm … which they did. She got the nickname Kate Bar-lass after that. There are still people in Scotland named Barlas after her – but don't ask them if it's because their granny worked in a bar![6]

Queen Joan

James I's wife, Joan, had the pleasure of capturing his killers and their leader, Walter, Earl of Atholl. She could have had him hanged, drawn and quartered, but she wanted a more savage revenge than that. She made his execution last three days. On the first day he had a rope tied round his feet and was hoisted in the air on a crane. The rope was allowed to drop towards the ground then it was stopped suddenly so his legs were pulled out of their sockets. He was then led off to a pillory and crowned with a red-hot iron crown that was stamped 'King of traitors'. On the second day he was dragged through the streets of Edinburgh, strapped to a stretcher that was tied to the tail of a horse. James I's loyal subjects could jeer and throw things at him. Only on the third day was he finally hanged, drawn and quartered. The message was 'Don't mess with Joan!'

Mary of Gueldres

James II's wife was a tough woman who went to war with him. When a cannon blew his head off she could have given up and gone home. Instead she carried on with the battle to take Roxburgh Castle and won it for her son, James III. She then led a force to capture other English castles at Wark and Norham. She went back home and built Ravenscraig Castle, the first Scottish castle to be built with extra-strength roofing to take cannon. After a series of boyfriends she fancied being a queen again so she proposed to Edward IV of England shortly before she died!

6 Some boring people say Kate Bar-lass wasn't even in the room at the time she was supposed to have struggled to save the king. Pity, because it's a good story!

SUFFERING SCHOOLS

In the Middle Ages in England and Wales it was tough at school.

Schools – the good news

You didn't have to go if you were poor ... or a girl.
Most boys only went to school from the ages of 7 to 14.
There was no homework.
There were no spelling corrections – you spelled English any way you wanted to.

Schools – the bad news

You had no break-times – only a short stop for lunch.
Make a mistake and you were beaten – usually with branches from a birch tree.
You had to buy your own paper, ink and books – which were very expensive.
And of course there were 'School Rules'...

Westminster School in the 13th century had the following rules...

Let them say prayers every morning without shouting

Let there be no grinning or chattering or laughing

Let them not make fun of another if he does not read or sing well

Let them not hit one another secretly

Let them not answer rudely if questioned by their elders

LET THOSE WHO BREAK THESE RULES FEEL THE ROD WITHOUT DELAY!

Not too bad so far? Not much different from your own school, apart from the bit about being hit with a rod!

Some of the other rules were really odd. But they must have needed these rules because someone actually did these dreadful deeds...

Anyone who has torn to pieces his school mate's bed or hidden the bedclothes or thrown shoes or pillow from corner to corner or thrown the school into disorder shall be severely punished in the morning.

No wonder this boy's 15th-century poem was so popular with pupils. He wrote about being late for school and giving a cheeky reply to his teacher...

My master looks like he is mad,
'Where have you been, my sorry lad?'
'Milking ducks my mother had!'
It is no wonder that I'm sad.

My master peppered my backside with speed,
It was worse than fennel seed;
He would not stop till it did bleed,
I'm truly sorry for his deed.

I wish my master was a hare,
And all his fat books hound dogs were.
Me, the hunter, I'd not spare
Him. If he died I would not care!

Why was the boy late? You might well ask. Well, school often began at five in the morning in summer time! Wouldn't you be late?

TERRIBLE TUDOR TIMES

T he Wars of the Roses in England came to a bloody end when a Welsh Prince Henry Tudor defeated Richard II in battle. He made himself King Henry VII of England, the first of the terrible Tudors.

TERRIBLE TIMELINE

1485

Richard III is hacked to death at the Battle of Bosworth Field. His Welsh opponent, Henry Tudor, is crowned Henry VII. This man is ruthless – and quite toothless too – but not utheless when it comes to money. He will make England rich.

1503

James IV of Scotland marries Margaret – Henry VII's daughter from England. That should unite the nations. Fat chance.

1520

Henry VIII sends some soldiers to tame the 'wild Irish' – the ones outside the Dublin 'Pale' – but Henry's too busy fighting the Scots, the French and various popes to get very far.

1534

Henry doesn't like being told what to do by the head of the Catholic Church, the Pope. Henry wants a divorce – Pope says, 'No.' Henry says, 'Right! I'll make my own Church of England and give myself a divorce.' This new 'Protestant' religion will cause untold misery in its struggle against the old Catholic Church. And English will kill and torture English, of course.

1536

Henry VIII makes Wales part of England with the 'Act of Union'. Henry's family was Welsh, of course, so this was not a very friendly thing for him to do. In the same year he has wife Anne Boleyn beheaded – so he's not a very friendly man after all.

1542

Scottish James V's troops lose to the English at Solway Moss and he dies of a broken heart. His 6-day-old daughter, Mary Queen of Scots, takes the crown (even though it's too big for her).

1567

Mary Queen of Scots is thrown off the throne and flees to England. She asks cousin Queen Elizabeth I of England to protect her. Liz 'protects' Mary for 19 years in prison! In Scotland her 13-month-old son, James VI, becomes king.

1587

Elizabeth I finally decides to execute Mary Queen of Scots for plotting to overthrow her. Liz says sorry to James, so that's all right.

1588

The Spanish Armada attacks England – and loses. Spanish survivors are shipwrecked in Ireland. They are mostly massacred ... by their friends, the 'wild Irish' peasants! The English won't get out of Ireland but haven't the power to crush it entirely. As Liz's governor says, 'I have often wished Ireland could be sunk in the sea.' Charming!

1590

The start of North Berwick witch-trials; torture and terror for many innocent people in Scotland. James VI of Scotland enjoys the torture and watches it being carried out. Kruel king.

1600

The English try a nasty new weapon – famine. They burn the Irish crops and stop the next year's being planted. By 1602, bodies lie in ditches, mouths stained green from trying to eat nettles.

1603

James VI of Scotland takes the throne of England too when Elizabeth dies. He becomes James I of England. Finally, one king for both countries. Peace at last? No chance.

Chop till you drop

The Tudor age was famous for its beheadings – two of Henry VIII's wives lost their noddles and so did Elizabeth I's cousin, Mary Queen of Scots. So did hundreds of others like the Countess of Salisbury – who gave the executioner a run for his money.

What would *you* do if an executioner said,

Would you do as you were told? Would you say, as you were supposed to, 'I forgive you, executioner,' and give him a bag of gold? Or would you be really rotten to the poor axeman like the crazy old Countess of Salisbury?

Henry VIII planned to visit York. He wanted the Tower of London empty of prisoners so none would escape while his back was turned. One of those prisoners was the Countess of Salisbury. When it was her turn to be executed, Henry's chief executioner, Master Cratwell, was away from London. The job was left to a boy. You have to feel sorry for him!

If the young executioner had written a letter home then it might have looked something like this…

Tower Green
London
1541

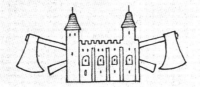

MINISTRY of EXECUTIONS

Dear Mum,

Started my new job as executioner today. It's not as easy as it looks! I have a nice uniform. Here's a picture I drew looking in a mirror...

You'd be proud of me — except you wouldn't know it was me cos Henry's executioners are ~~anommynus~~ ~~annunnymous~~ ~~ammeniass~~ secret.

Anyway the boss, Robert Cratwell (whose name I can't tell you cos it's secret), said I could start with an easy one. 'It's the old Countess of Salisbury,' he said. 'She's nearly seventy years old so she'll be no trouble.'

'Seventy!' I said. 'If she gets any older her head'll probably just drop off!' I laughed. I didn't know the joke would be on me! 'What's the old trout done?' I asked.

'Nothing,' Robert said. 'She's never had a trial or been found guilty. But her son, Cardinal Pole, was a Catholic and he started stirring up trouble for the king. So Henry had the Cardinal's old mother thrown in the tower a couple of years ago. And the king made sure she suffered in there with terrible food and no heating. The old woman will be glad to be out of it.'

Then he gave me a few last-minute lessons in chopping and sent me off to do some target-practice on a turnip. I was spot on. That turnip was sliced as neat as one that you put in your stew, mum. But there was no one watching was there? And turnips don't move.

Imagine the shock when I found a hundred and fifty people gathered round the scaffold! I was shaking with nerves, I can tell you. 'Would you mind putting your head on the block?' I asked her, ever so polite, just the way you taught me.

MINISTRY OF EXECUTIONS

Blow me, but the old woman says, 'No! A traitor would put their head on the block, but I'm not a traitor, so I won't!'

Her two guards grabbed her and held her down on her knees. But she was struggling all the time. They couldn't hold her head down because I'd have cut their hands off. That means she could still move her head around. Then she looks up at me and says, 'Catch me if you can.' She started bobbing and weaving and I started chopping. Well, I made a right mess of her shoulders before I finally got her in the neck and finished her off.

It was my job to hold up the head and cry, 'Behold the head of a traitor!' I was that scared I think I said, 'Behold the head of a tater!' The crowd were booing and throwing things at me. It was awful, Mum.

But Robert's back now and I'm getting extra lessons. In the meantime I'm working away in the torture chamber. They don't mind if you're clumsy in there and you don't have a big audience.

Give my love to the kids and the cat. I'll be home next week to help with chopping the firewood.

Love,

Your little Georgie

It's not known what happened to the boy executioner – but his master, Cratwell, was later hanged for robbery!

The good news is that horrible Henry VIII died of a slow disease. His legs had ulcers – open sores that had to be bandaged to stop them dripping all over the place. The Countess of Salisbury's death was messy … but Henry's was long, slow and painful. It's hard to feel sorry for him.

Horrible Highlands

Invasions haven't always been England invading its neighbours, of course. The Scots spent a lot of time attacking the English. It didn't always go to plan.

Scotland is really three countries rolled into one, of course.[7] There are the Borders to the south, the Lowlands in the middle and the Highlands in the north.

If Scotland has been battered and beaten in battles it is probably because these three regions haven't been working together.

At the Battle of Flodden, in 1513, the Scots invaded England while King Henry VIII was away fighting in France. Sneaky James IV of Scotland.

But it was said the Highlanders wanted to have a quick raid, steal some cattle then go home.

WE WEREN'T PREPARED TO HANG AROUND AND WAIT FOR THE ENGLISH TO MARCH TO THE BORDERS. MIND YOU, THE ONES WHO STAYED AND FOUGHT WITH THEIR DOUBLE-HANDED SWORDS WERE DEADLY

Too many Highlanders went home and left King James IV without the help of their battle swords.

Meanwhile the Lowland Scots were fighting with pikes – three times the height of a man. The pikes were a present from their French friends, but useless for a British battle.

WHEN WE CHARGED WE TRIPPED OVER THEM. THE ENGLISH JUST SLICED THROUGH THE WOODEN SHAFTS AND LEFT US HOLDING A USELESS LUMP OF WOOD. WE WERE SLAUGHTERED

At the same battle the Border soldiers knew the English Bordermen well. They were neighbours. So they didn't try very hard to kill them.

MOST OF US HAVE BROTHERS AND SISTERS MARRIED INTO FAMILIES ON THE OTHER SIDE OF THE BORDER. WE WAVED OUR LANCES THEN SET ABOUT OUR REAL BUSINESS – ROBBING THE BODIES ON THE BATTLEFIELD. AND WE DIDN'T CARE IF THEY WERE SCOTTISH OR ENGLISH BODIES

No wonder poor James lost – three regions fighting three different types of battle.

---

7 Or four if you count the Orkneys and Shetland which have been affected by contact with Scandinavian countries.

NOSHING BRITS

You may think school dinners are bad. Look at what people ate in the past and stop complaining.

EATING BITS OF BRITS

Brits have battered each other about a bit.[8] But have they ever eaten each other? There are some stories that say they have...

ROMAN AND CHIPS

The Romans built Hadrian's Wall around AD 130. It separated the Roman English lands from the Scots. But one Scottish tribe scared the Romans more than any other: the Attacotti who lived near Glasgow. St Jerome wrote in around AD 410...

> A fearless tribe of Scotland, the Attacotti, are accused of enjoying the taste of human flesh. When they hunted the woods for prey, it is said that they attacked the shepherd rather than his flock. They curiously selected the brain, both of males and females, which they cooked for their horrid meals.

DON'T WORRY WE JUST WANT TO PICK YOUR BRAINS

ANYONE WANT SHEPHERD'S THIGH?

HUNGER HORRORS

In Saxon England you grew food in summer and ate it over the winter. But if you failed to grow the food in the summer then you starved over winter.

What would stop you growing food in summer?

- Bad weather, heavy rain, floods from the sea or storms destroying your wheat
- Viking invaders burning your fields and stealing your cattle
- Plague (killing off farm workers) and animal plagues destroying your flocks

WE'RE IN FOR A TOUGH WINTER

That's what happened a few times in Saxon England. What could you do if you were a starving Saxon? Jump off a cliff or eat your neighbours? Does that sound daft? Well they're horribly historically true, as the chronicles of the time tell...

8 The have also battered a lot of cod. Some Brits worship their cod. They go to churches and sing hymns like, 'Nearer my Cod to thee', 'Oh Cod our Help in Ages Past' and 'Holy, Holy, Holy! Lord Cod Almighty'.

THE FAMINE FOOD GUIDE

Crops failed? Got a rumbling tum? Then try these top tips from the Saxon Chronicle and see how you can cure those hunger pains!

FALL IN LINE

In Sussex last year forty villagers cured their hunger for good. They went to the edge of a cliff, joined hands and jumped over. The ones who weren't crushed on the rocks were drowned in the sea. Fast food for fish!

FUNERAL FOOD

It's been reported that when villagers died in a famine area they were not buried by their families (as that would be a waste of good meat). Instead they were cooked and eaten. Human hotpot saves lives.

SLAVE AWAY

The Saxon law says: 'A father may sell a son if that child is under seven years old and if he needs to do so.' Selling children earns you money ... and, remember, you save because you don't have to feed them! No kids is good kids – no kidding!

FOR SALE

GOOD LORD!

It is a lord of the manor's duty to protect his people. If the worst comes to the worst, visit your local lord, kneel in front of him and place your head in his hands. You then become his slave and work for him – but at least he'll feed you. Lords of manors means good manners!

TREE-MENDOUS!

When all else fails you can eat anything in sight. It's been reported that Saxon survivors ground up food – from acorns to tree-bark, nettles and wild grass to fill out the flour. Your bark can be good for your bite!

The Saxons also ate all the dogs, cats and rats in the village.

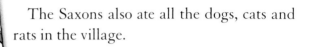

STEAK AND KID PIE

The Irish writer Jonathan Swift lived from 1667 till 1745 and his most famous book is 'Gulliver's Travels'. But his most shocking writing was an article he wrote called 'A modest proposal' in which he said...

The Irish peasants are poor and starving because they have too many children to feed and too little land. The English, on the other hand, have plenty of money and are greedy for fresh meat.

The answer is so simple I am amazed that no one has suggested it before. The Irish peasants should sell their children to the English and the English can buy them to eat!

I have been told that a young, healthy child of a year old is a most delicious, nourishing and wholesome food, whether it's stewed, roasted, baked or boiled. I humbly suggest that 100,000 infants may be offered for sale to rich people in the kingdom. The mothers should try to make sure that they are plump and fat and good for the table.

Of course Swift was joking ... but a few horrified people believed him. They probably shared a brain with a dung beetle.

HORRIBLE HAGGIS

Scotland is now famous for the 'haggis' pudding. Popular poet Robbie Burns wrote 'To a Haggis' – sadly the haggis never wrote back.

Burns called the haggis the 'great chieftain of the puddin' race'. Here's a quick guide to how it used to be made – it's a lot cleaner these days! But try the old method if you fancy chomping on the real chieftain...

HAGGIS
SCOTTISH SUPER SUPPER

1 First kill your sheep. (If you haven't any beef suet handy then you may have to kill a cow as well.)

2 Cut out the sheep's heart, its liver, its lungs and its stomach. Turn the stomach inside out to clean it of all that half-chewed grass (not to mention the crunched beetles that were living on the grass and the sheep-droppings that the sheep accidentally sucked up).

3 Meanwhile pop the heart, liver and lungs into some boiling, salted water. (If you get bored waiting for them to cook, then take the sheep's wool and knit yourself a kilt.)

4 When it's all nicely cooked then mince it all together. (I hope you remembered to wash your hands.)

5 Stir in salt, pepper, nutmeg, cayenne and a chopped onion. Then add a pound of chopped beef suet, oatmeal and a cup of gravy. Mix it all together. (Keep stirring till it looks like a hedgehog after the fifteenth lorry has run over it.)

6 Stuff the sheep's stomach with the mixture. (Remember to stitch up one end before you start packing it in the other end otherwise there'll be a mess on the floor.)

7 Boil the pudding in a large pan of water for three hours. (You'll be getting hungry by now. That's all right – you'll enjoy the haggis all the more when you get to eat it, so keep your hands off that bag of crisps.)

8 Invite your favourite teacher to dinner. (Or, even better, the teacher who gave you the worst report in the universe.)

9 Serve the haggis on a well-starched napkin. (A handkerchief that you've just blown your nose on will not do.)

10 Watch your guest eat the haggis with chappit tatties and bashed neeps (that's mashed potato and mashed swede to you ignorant readers) – and, while they're eating, tell them what's inside!

You might like to recite a couple of lines of Robbie Burns's 'Selkirk Grace' before your guest tucks in. Burns said some people have food but can't eat it, other people need food but can't get any. He ends…

> *But we hae[9] meat and we can eat,*
> *And so the lord be thankit.*

9 'hae' is Scots for 'have'.

SLIMY STUART TIMES

Elizabeth I, the last Tudor, was dying. Just before she popped her clogs she said the next king should be James VI of Scotland. He went down to London and became James I of England. The poor English will never get to rule themselves.

TERRIBLE TIMELINE

1603
James wants Scotland to join England and Wales and have one government. That is not a popular idea and he has to scrap it. Back home, with no English to fight, the Highlanders turn on one another in a raid called 'the Slaughter of Lennox'.

1605
The Catholics hoped James would be a better king for them than the Tudors. He wasn't, so they planned to blow him up. Guy Fawkes was taken in front of James and the plotter confessed it had been his hope to blow James and his family back to Scotland.

1609
The Plantation starts in Ireland. James I's plan is to take Ulster (the north-east corner of Ireland) from the native Irish (who are Catholics). They send in English and Scots (who are Protestants) as farmers. Four hundred years later this is still causing problems.

1616
The playwright William Shakespeare dies on his 52nd birthday. That probably spoiled the party a bit.

1642
King Charles I and the posh Cavaliers get into a Civil War against the English Parliament and their supporters, the Roundheads.

1647

Charles escapes from England after losing the Civil War. He runs home to Scotland. Silly boy. The Scots sell him back to the English.

1649

Parliament is now dominated by its army under General Oliver Cromwell who makes sure Charlie the chump loses. The Roundheads have Charlie executed. England is ruled by Oliver Cromwell – an Englishman!

1649

Oliver Cromwell arrives in Ireland. He doesn't mess about with revolting Catholics, he massacres lots of them. He stays just nine months yet his horrors will be remembered in Ireland for hundreds of years.

1658

Cromwell dies. The English invite chopped Charlie's son, Charles II, to take his dad's throne. Cromwell's body is dug up, cut up and thrown in the River Thames while his head is stuck on a pole at Westminster Hall for 25 years.

1665

The Great Plague. In London alone 100,000 people die ... and just as many rats. Then, a year later, the Great Fire of London destroys a lot of the filthy slums that gave homes to the rats that spread the plague.

1679

Titus Oates spreads wild stories about a Catholic plot to kill the king. As a result several Catholics are executed horribly. In Cardiff, Wales, the priests John Lloyd and Philip Evans are butchered cruelly at Cardiff Castle on 22 July.

People were paid to say they were traitors. Evans heard of his death-sentence and sang with joy as he played his harp. He was sure he'd go to heaven ... and be playing harps with angels.

1688

King James II is a Catholic and hopes an army of Irish Catholics will help him keep the throne of England and Scotland. The Irish Protestants in Derry fear this Catholic army has arrived to massacre them. Apprentice boys[10] pinch the keys to the city and lock the gates. A victory that will cause a lot of grief in later years. James is thrown off the throne. Even his daughter, Mary, is glad to see the back of him. She takes over with hubby, William of Orange.

10 These days we call them 'teenagers' – they were boys who had left school and were learning a job.

1691

Battle of Aughrim sees 7,000 Irish slaughtered and their general lose his head to a cannonball. The Treaty of Limerick puts the Protestants in charge. The Catholics are suppressed. By 1704 they can't vote ... or go to school, so it's not all bad news.

1692

What do Scots do when they've no English to fight? Attack each other. Famous Glencoe Massacre this year. The Campbell clan kill the Macdonalds – well, it makes a change from killing the English.

1707

England has shared its Parliament with Wales since 1536 (when a Welsh Tudor was ruling). Now, a hundred years after having a Scottish king, it finally gets around to sharing its Parliament with the old enemy, Scotland. At last we have 'Great Britain'. In 1801 Ireland will join to make 'The United Kingdom of Great Britain and Ireland'.

Hunger horrors

In 1602, the Irish suffered horribly when the English burned their crops and stopped the next year's crops being planted.

One of the tales to come out of the famine was of an old lady who lived near Newry in the north-east of Ireland.

Are you sitting comfortably, children? Then I'll tell you her terrible tale...

Once upon a time there were two poor hungry children who lived on a farm. There was no food for the family and no food for the chickens or cows or sheep or pigs. First the cow died and the little girl cried. But that night the children had cow meat in their soup.

So when the sheep died the little girl didn't cry very much. And when the pig died she didn't cry at all! After a week with no food, the children's father died and they buried him in a shallow grave at the edge of the wood.

After another week without food, the children's mother died. 'I'm too weak to bury her,' the boy said.

The girl sighed and said, 'You wouldn't be weak if you had some stew! I'll make you some!'

And the girl made some stew for her brother. 'This is very tasty, sister!' The boy sighed. 'Where did you get the meat?' And the girl smiled and said nothing.

The boy went off to bury his mother. When he returned an hour later, he shook his head and said, 'When I buried her I noticed a strange thing. Mother had one leg missing! Where can it have gone?'

And his sister smiled and said nothing. She just licked her lips.

After another week with no food the boy ran into the house calling, 'Sister! Sister! There's a fire outside the old woman's cottage on the edge of the wood! She must have some food! Let's go and ask her for some!'

So the two children ran across the fields till they came to the little turf cottage. The woman was as thin and wrinkled as a chicken's leg. 'Welcome my little friends! I am so happy to see you!' The old woman grinned and her rotten teeth sparkled in the firelight.

'Have you any dinner?' The boy said.

The woman drew a gleaming knife from behind her back. 'I have now!' she cackled. 'I have now!'

The story of children eating their dead mother is true, and so is the tale of the old woman luring children to their death with fires.

History as horrible as Hansel and Gretel.

Wicked witch-hunters

People have been accused of witchcraft for thousands of years – they're even mentioned in the Bible. In AD 840 a law was passed that said a witch should be punished by having his or her tongue cut out.

In later years they were taken to the stake and strangled. In Scotland strangling was known as 'wirrying'.

The body was then burned. Of course this was a little bit kinder than being burned alive – but not much. (The kind-hearted English never burned a single witch – but they hanged hundreds of them!)

James the sick Sixth

The worst of the witch-hunts were in the 1500s and the 1600s. Sadly and madly, King James VI of Scotland was a great believer in witchcraft. He wrote a very thick (and very stupid) book on the subject.

He was quite sure that people were out to kill him with witchcraft and went along to witch trials to see what went on. Would you get a fair trial with James there? You had more chance of seeing the Loch Ness monster on water skis.

First you'd be tortured. Which would you prefer?

James VI went to the trial of a man accused of witchcraft. First he watched as the man had his fingernails torn out with pliers.

Then James saw the Boot being used on the man. A report says the victim's leg was crushed so badly, 'the blood and marrow spurted out'. Still the man would not confess.

The last witch

In Dundee there is a story that they burned a witch called Grissel Jaffrey – without 'wirrying' her first. The local legend says…

A young sailor stepped ashore at Dundee and saw a crowd of people round the market cross. He had been born in the town but had been away for many years. When he asked them what was going on they told him that a witch was about to be burned. He decided to stay and watch before going home to see his old parents.

The fire was lit and the old woman screamed that she was innocent. Through the flames the sailor saw that the victim at the stake was his own mother. He left the town, cursing it and vowing never to return.

Everyone in Dundee believes the story of Grissel Jaffrey, but historians have checked the records of the courts and the church and there is no mention of a witch trial in 1669. The church leaders say the people made it up.

But an old history of Dundee copies a passage from the records of the town council. It says clearly that Grissel Jaffrey was burned after confessing to witchcraft. Not only that but she named other witches in the town.

That history book was written in 1874. The writer saw the record for himself. The record is no longer there. Where has it gone?

Disappeared through witchcraft?

Or removed by people who are ashamed of what the Dundee church did? Which do you think?

❧ DID YOU KNOW…? ❧

The Scottish church court was very annoyed when King George II of England and Scotland scrapped all the witchcraft laws in 1735. After all, they'd burned their last witch just eight years before and were ready to burn more if they found them.

GORY GEORGIAN BRITAIN

In Georgian Britain there were lots of revolutions going on. Some Scots wanted their Stuart family back on the throne, so they invaded England – and lost.
The Americans wanted to be free of the British rule – they won. The French copied the Americans and sent their king to the guillotine. The Irish copied the French – and lost.
It seems everyone was revolting.

TERRIBLE TIMELINE

1714
George I comes from Hanover (Germany) to take the English throne. He's not popular, but he's Protestant and the other Stuarts are Catholics and most Brits don't want that.

1715
Stuart supporters want James III to rule so they have a rebellion in support of him – these 'Jacobite' rebellions are crushed ... for the moment.

1728
The first of four dreadful Irish famines in the 1700s. The peasants live in poverty while the posh Protestants build Dublin into a grand city as fine as London. The Protestant power is known as the 'Ascendancy' – and of course it makes the peasants jealous and rebellious. Wouldn't you be?

1745
The Jacobites are revolting again. They want the old Stuarts back on the throne. Bonnie Prince Charlie leads their rebellion – he's not very bonnie but he looks a complete Charlie when his tartan army is crushed at the Battle of Culloden in 1746. The last great battle on British soil.

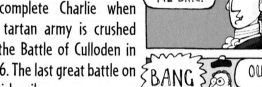

1770
Captain Cook claims Australia for Britain. (He doesn't bother to ask the Aborigines if they want to be British, of course.) Britain needs the extra land because the old dumping ground for crooks, America, rebels in 1775.

1780
Gordon Riots. Now an English lord is leading riots (against the Catholics this time). Lord George Gordon heads the

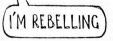

riots that go on for a week. Five hundred people are hurt. The mob tear holes in a prison roof, and captives escape. Londoners barricaded themselves in their homes. The escaping prisoners rattle their chains at them. Creepy.

1788

Australia welcomes its first British convicts. It's a good place to dump them. And only 48 died on the voyage!

1793

The French have chopped their King Louis' head off with the guillotine. Now they are looking for a fight and pick on Britain. This is the start of twenty years of wars – the Napoleonic Wars. And the French Revolution gives the Irish ideas...

1798

Wolfe Tone leads United Irishmen in a rising which is crushed. Apart from getting 30,000 people killed it gets Ireland's parliament abolished (the English decided it can't be trusted). Ireland will be ruled directly from London for the next century.

1801

Ireland joins Great Britain and another red cross is added to the flag to make the Union Jack.

1804

Captain Dick's puffer starts running! The first steam railway locomotive is invented by Richard Trevithick, and it runs in Wales. Within a hundred years it'll be goodbye to horse-power and hello to trains and cars. Hedgehogs will pay the price.

1822

Now the Welsh are revolting. Miners form themselves into gangs called the 'Scotch Cattle'. Their aim is to stop strangers coming along and taking their jobs. Mainly the Irish who were starving in Ireland. The Irish would work for low wages and put the Welsh miners out of jobs. The Scotch Cattle gangs set out to drive the strangers away. They blacken their faces and wear head-dresses with bulls' horns on them. It leads to murder of course.

Cruel Culloden

The last battle ever to be fought on British soil was, of course, between the old enemies England and Scotland. The Scots wanted to be ruled by their Bonnie Prince Charlie – one of the old Stuart family – and he led a rebellion with the help of England's old enemies ... the French. The final battle was at Culloden near Inverness.

It ended in victory for the English, led by the Duke of Cumberland. If a newspaper had been written about it at the time, then it may have read like this...

Charlie's Champs meet the Butcher Boys today at Culloden and some people are saying it will be the decider in this long-running contest. But will it be cheers for Charlie and curtains for Cumberland? Or a Bonnie Prince bloodbath and a battering by the Butcher? Our experts have been looking at the strengths and weaknesses of the two sides. If you want to get down to the betting shop and make your fortune then here are our top ten tips for today from our reporter on the scene..

THE CULLODEN CRUNCH

	CHARLIE'S CLANS	SCORE
NUMBERS	5,000 at the last count. The Frasers and Mackenzies are on their way but our experts say they'll arrive too late. If he waits a day he'll have another 3,500.	5
STRENGTH	There are no stronger men in the British Isles. But these men have only eaten one biscuit each in the last day or so. A serious handicap. The fighters are awesome men, but there are old men and boys behind them who are quite feeble.	4
TACTICS	The Clans prefer sudden attacks from the hills. They are not at their best in an open battle like this. As a result they tried an attack on the Redcoats before dawn. They got lost in the dark and failed. This open ground is good for cannon. Pity the Prince has so few!	3
FITNESS	After that night raid the Clansmen are exhausted and sleeping. The generals advise the Prince to give them a day's rest. He refuses. Many of the men fall asleep on the wet heather. They are cold, tired and hungry.	4
WEAPONS	Many men have lost their shields. They have few cannon and poor horses. The cannon they do have are pointing downhill which makes them difficult to fire. And the gunners aren't too well trained.	5
COURAGE	The Highlanders would charge at the mouth of a cannon to prove their courage. But their leaders are not so brave. They believe the position is desperate. Even the Prince is losing heart.	7
LOYALTY	The men are united by their hatred for the English, but not much else. Prince Charles has upset many Clan leaders because he insists he is the commander.	7
LEADERSHIP	Charles is too proud to take advice and too foolish to see the problems for himself.	6
SPIRIT	Don't forget the Jacobites are defending an unbeaten home record. They are fighting for their lives and their homes as well as their Prince. But this heavy rain seems to be depressing them.	7
BATTLEFIELD	Prince Charles refused permission for his officers to check the ground. He doesn't know his men will have to charge through a swamp before they even reach the enemy.	4
TOTAL		52

By Calvin McSlippery

BUTCHER'S ARMY	SCORE
,000–10,000 well-trained men. Many of them have fought throughout Europe for ears and are well organized.	10
hese men are well fed and fighting is their career. Yesterday was Cumberland's irthday – he treated them all to bread, cheese and brandy. Still, a ten-mile walk to the attlefield this morning will have tired them.	6
annon will mow down hundreds of Scots before they charge. The Redcoats will form nto three rows with muskets and simply wait for a Highland charge. When a soldier's hot is fired he still has a bayonet on the end of his gun.	7
umberland knows the Clans are exhausted. He is moving his men forward now so the nemy have no chance to rest. His own men were in bed by 10 last night and ready at a.m. this morning.	7
hey have well-organized rows of cannon. They'll fire twenty shots to the Highlanders' ne. And the bayonet practice has been very useful. The rain is bad news for keeping he firelocks on their muskets dry.	7
hey have a bad record against the Clansmen. Faced by a charge they have been forced o flee several times before now. They have a new way of fighting with bayonets that nay work against the dreaded Highland charge.	4
umberland has spoken to his men and said that if any were afraid to face the Scots then hey could go now and they would not be punished. No one goes. They trust him.	7
umberland is ruthless but his men know he is in charge and are as afraid of him as they re of the enemy. He is fearless in a battle.	8
hey are eager to repay past defeats and to fight against men they see as traitors. They on't think the Highlanders should be making war when Britain is already at war with rance. They are angry and full of vengeance.	6
his is the sort of battle they are used to. They have time to line up in rows, place their annon on firm ground and have a clear plan of action.	9
	71

The battle wasn't simply between English and Scots. There were many Scots fighting for Cumberland – they did not like the idea of being ruled by Charlie. Both armies followed bagpipes into battle. There were Irish and English fighting for Charlie.

Cumberland's cannon punched great gaps in the lines of Highlanders and drove Bonnie Prince Charlie off the battlefield. When the Highlanders charged forward they were brilliantly brave and hopelessly lost. It was a massacre and it lasted barely three-quarters of an hour.

Culloden was the last battle to be fought on British soil. It was also one of the most brutal. The Duke of Cumberland gave orders that there should be no prisoners taken. The wounded who were left on the battlefield were murdered. There are even stories of Highland prisoners being burned alive.

The really tragic thing was that it was only the start of the government's campaign to clear these Highland troublemakers out once and for all. It was the end of the Jacobite rebellions and the start of the 'Clearances'.

Diary of a rebellion

The French had a revolution in the 1790s that got rid of their unpopular king. The Irish decided this was a good idea. A man called Wolfe Tone founded 'The Society of United Irishmen' to start a rebellion.

They were mostly Protestants, who hated being bossed by the English as much as the Catholics did. The Society of United Irishmen met in Belfast and had a really good idea...

In 1798 they sent Wolfe Tone to France in disguise, to ask for help...

The French sent 43 ships to land at Bantry Bay, Cork ... but the wind drove them back to France. Meanwhile the defenders (mainly Irish Catholics) set about seeking and destroying the United Irishmen.

Flogging was a popular way to make prisoners betray the rebels ... but, as witnesses said...

Some stood the torture to the last gasp rather than betray their friends. Others did not, and one single informer in the town was enough to destroy all the United Irishmen in it.

I saw a man being flogged until his flesh was torn to shreds, begging to be shot.

Men were flogged until their spines, ribs and livers could be seen.

The rebellion of United Irishmen broke out in May 1798. The rebels hoped to attack Dublin under the cover of darkness by getting the lamplighters to go on strike, but soldiers with prodding bayonets persuaded the lamplighters to go to work!

In Wexford the rebels, led by a priest, Father John Murphy, had an early success. They defeated men from Cork who pleaded for their lives ... in Irish.

At Enniscorthy to the north of Wexford the rebels captured 35 enemy soldiers at Vinegar Hill and shut them in a windmill. The prisoners made a huge mistake. They complained…

WE'RE OVERCROWDED!

The rebels soon sorted that little problem for them…

TAKE A DOZEN OUT AND STAB THEM TO DEATH WITH YOUR PIKES

But by June, Vinegar Hill had been taken and Father John Murphy captured. He had a brutal execution (what did you expect?)…

FIRST HANG HIM THEN CUT OFF HIS HEAD AND STICK IT ON A POLE. HIS BODY SHOULD BE BURNED IN A TAR BARREL!

GULP!

In August 1798 the French finally invaded – too late and too little with just 1,000 men. And Wolfe Tone was captured. He was sentenced to hang. On the morning of his execution he was found to have cut his windpipe with a penknife, but failed to cut the artery that would have let him bleed to death. The execution was put off.

After a week in agony, a surgeon told Tone that if he tried to speak it would kill him. Tone replied…

I CAN STILL FIND A WORD TO THANK YOU, SIR. IT IS THE MOST WELCOME NEWS YOU COULD GIVE ME

Then he died.

But the rebellion wasn't quite over. Some United Irishmen who fled to Paris started it up again in 1803, led by Robert Emmet – another Protestant, by the way. His rebellion was a miserable failure where 80 men turned up to take Dublin Castle with just one ladder.

Emmet was hanged, but not as a glorious hero. He asked the hangman…

DO NOT TURN ME OFF TILL I DROP MY HANDKERCHIEF

…but he wouldn't drop it! In the end the hangman grew fed up with Emmet saying, 'Not yet!' And he pushed him off…

I HAVEN'T DROPPED MY HANDKERCHOKE!

CRIMINAL BRITS

Britain has always had some cruel criminals – and it still has. But in the past the punishments were far more cruel than the crimes. Just be glad you didn't live in the painful past.

WHIPS AND LIPS

Life was tough for law-breakers in the Dark Ages. Saxons could be savage.

Traitors, outlaws, witches, wizards and frequent thieves could all receive the death penalty.

But the execution method varied from place to place, time to time and crime to crime. If you were caught, how would you like to go? Which of these Saxon punishments would you choose to suffer?

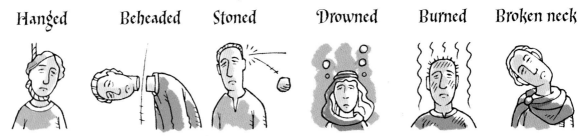

Hanged   Beheaded   Stoned   Drowned   Burned   Broken neck

None of those?

All right. A merciful Saxon judge may teach you a lesson with a bit of mutilation – that is he'd have bits cut off you. Which could you do without…?

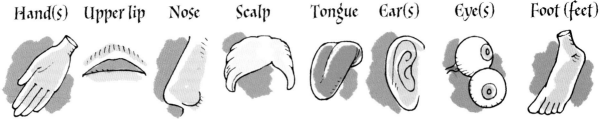

Hand(s)   Upper lip   Nose   Scalp   Tongue   Ear(s)   Eye(s)   Foot (feet)

None of those either? Then you could be…

You'd rather go to prison?

Sorry – there may be a cellar in the lord's manor house to hold you for a short while, but no prisons.

Branded with a hot iron   Put in the stocks   Whipped

68

Painful punishments

Henry II of England (1133–1189) tried to make modern laws but the punishments for breaking them were still very old fashioned.

THE ATTACKER

NAME: Thomas of Elderfield
CRIME: Fought against George of Northway and did wound him.
PUNISHMENT: Sentenced to fight a duel with George. He was defeated, and the law demands that Thomas's eyes be gouged out by George's family.

(It is said that Thomas was nursed back to health by St Wulfstan in Worcester. His eyes were miraculously restored!)

THE THIEF

NAME: Peter of Clarendon
CRIME: Felony. He did steal a horse to the value of two shillings.
PUNISHMENT: The Sheriff of Wiltshire had a pit dug and filled with water which was then blessed by a priest. The thief was thrown in. If he sank he was innocent. Peter of Clarendon floated and was therefore guilty. He was taken out and executed.

(Sheriff Ranulf Glanville of Yorkshire killed 120 men in this way.)

THE SCOLD

NAME: Ann Runcorn
CRIME: She did disgrace her husband by scolding him in public, calling him 'villain' and 'rogue'.
PUNISHMENT: Ann was fitted with a cage over her head – an instrument called a 'brank'. A metal rod poked into her mouth to hold down her tongue. Ann had to sit on a horse facing backwards, and be led through the market where people could mock her.

(A brank in the town of Shrewsbury was last used in 1846.)

THE FORGER

NAME: John Stubbs
CRIME: He did make copies of the king's coins and used the forged coins to buy food.
PUNISHMENT: John Stubbs' hand was tied to a block of wood. A meat axe was placed on his wrist and struck with a hammer till the hand was cut off.

(Amputation of a hand was a rare punishment but the law was still in force in 1820.)

THE BEGGAR

NAME: Martin of Cheapside
CRIME: He did beg for money when fit and able to work.
PUNISHMENT: Three days and three nights in the stocks in the marketplace, fed on only bread and water. He was then thrown out of the town and ordered not to return.

(The kind Tudors reduced this punishment to one day and night in the stocks in 1504.)

THE LIAR

NAME: John de Hackford
CRIME: In 1364 he falsely announced that 10,000 men were gathering to murder the London councillors. This caused widespread fear and panic.
PUNISHMENT: He was jailed for a year. Every three months he was taken out, stood in a pillory (or stretch-neck) with a stone round his neck and a notice 'False Liar' pinned to his chest.

THE HAWK FINDER

NAME: John of Rivers
CRIME: He did find his lordship's hawk on the roof of his house. He failed to report this to his lordship.
PUNISHMENT: The hawk shall be fed on six ounces of flesh cut from John of Rivers' chest.

Sick surgeons

Surgeons needed to know how the human body worked, so they would cut up corpses to dig around and have a look.

The law said they could only use the bodies of criminals who'd been executed. The trouble is there weren't enough to keep the cutters happy. So they started pinching fresh corpses from graveyards in the 1700s and early 1800s.

In Liverpool in 1826 the police found eleven corpses pickled in barrels and ready to be shipped off to the surgeons. (The body-snatchers went to prison for 12 months each.)

The good news is you could stop them digging up your granny! Here's how …

Are YOU worried by

BODY SNATCHERS???

Afraid your dearly beloved will be

GRABBED FROM THE GRAVE…
…OR SNATCHED FROM THE SOIL
…OR CLUTCHED FROM THE COFFIN?

Worried they may not rest in peace…
…but in pieces on the surgeon's slab???

Then why not hire the Pannal Stone?
This huge boulder will be placed over
your loved one's grave by our expert stone shifters.

It will stay there two weeks till the
corpse is too rotten to interest the surgeon.

Write to: Pannal Stone Hire Ltd, Leadgate Road, Harrogate for details.
Remember…

BETTER STONED THAN BONED!!!

The Pannal Stone can still be seen in the graveyard at Pannal.

At Woodplumpton in Lancashire there is a boulder too. But it isn't there to keep the body-snatchers out. It's there to keep Meg Shelton IN. She was said to be a witch. Meg could not rest after death and clawed her way out … three times. So the fourth time they put the boulder on top.

It would have been easier to just bury her face down.

Hare-raising horror

The two most famous Scottish 'body snatchers' were called Burke and Hare… But they never 'snatched' a single body!

They ran a cheap and filthy hotel for the poor in Edinburgh. When Burke and Hare found a poor person with no friends or relatives they would offer them a bed for the night.

Nice men? No. They would suffocate the victim and sell the body.

Burke and Hare weren't really *body snatchers*, they were murderers. They were caught, and in 1829 Burke was hanged.

Hare went free because he went to court and put all the blame on his old friend Burke.

Would you do that to your friend?

GRUESOME GARROTTERS

IN THE 1850S AND 1860S A NEW TERROR HIT THE CITY STREETS - GARROTTING. A VICTORIAN VILLAIN EXPLAINED TO OUR HORRIBLE HISTORIES REPORTER...

VICIOUS VICTORIAN BRITAIN

The Victorian Brits were clever people. They invented lots of new machines. Trains that could crush you far faster than the old carts. Machine guns to massacre people faster, and filthy factories that could give you deadly diseases. A lovely time to live.

TERRIBLE TIMELINE

1845
A disease rots most of the potatoes in Ireland and the people starve. The Irish Potato Famine kills over two million. Another two million move out of the country to find a new life somewhere else.

1846
Two thousand people a week are dying in the latest attack of cholera disease. You get diarrhoea, turn blue, and die. With 40,000 people in Liverpool living in crowded cellars it's no surprise.

1848
Young Ireland rebellion. Ends with the glorious 'Battle of Widow McCormack's Cabbage Garden'. Two rebels die and the posh Protestant rebel leader, William Smith O'Brien, is arrested. End of revolt.

1854
Britain is at war with Russia in the Crimea. Florence Nightingale patches them up.

1888
Jack the Ripper strikes in gloomy London streets. He kills eight women but is never caught. Don't worry girls – he is either a) about 150 years old or b) dead. Either way, you're safe.

1891
Now education is free for everyone. You all have to go to school, whether you want to or not! You'll be caned if you don't go – and probably caned if you do go. It's tough being a Victorian kid.

Chartists

In the 1820s the poor people of Britain decided they wanted the right to vote. They formed a group called the Chartists.

They were led by an Irishman and had a lot of support in Wales. They wanted to be peaceful – but of course it came to a messy end.

On 4 November 1839 the Chartists marched down Stow Hill in Newport, South Wales.

The army was waiting for them in the Westgate Hotel. No one knows who fired the first shot but a battle took place and over 20 Chartists died. A newspaper report of the time made gruesome reading. The local paper, the 'Monmouthshire Merlin' wrote…

many who suffered in the fight crawled away, some showing frightful wounds and glaring eyes wildly crying for mercy and seeking shelter from the people; others desperately maimed were carried for medical aid, and a few of the miserable objects that were helplessly and mortally wounded continued to writhe in torture, showing in their gory agonies a dismal and impressive example of what happens to rebels and a sickening and sad spectacle for the eye of the loyal people.

Nine dead Chartists were placed in the yard of the inn and made a deplorable sight. Many of the inhabitants of the town went to see them. A young woman forced her way through the crowd of spectators in the yard no sooner saw the dead than she uttered a heart-rendering shriek and threw herself upon one of the bodies. The gush of fondness and of sorrow was great. She was dragged from the man she loved, the blood of the fallen rioter having smeared her face and arms.

Foul famine

The good news for the poorest peasants in Ireland was that potatoes grew well in their fields. By the 1840s the most popular variety of spud was 'lumper' or 'horse potato'. It grew on the poorest land and gave a huge crop.

You just planted your potatoes in April and May, picked them in August, then they could be stored and eaten until the following May. During summer your family had to buy oatmeal to eat

until the next crop of spuds – this was the 'summer hunger' but it wasn't too bad. Some potatoes could be fed to your family pigs and they'd give you a bit of meat.

With the help of this super spud the population rose from 4.5 million in 1800 to 8 million in 1845. That was the good news. But the bad news was that you had no savings, because any spare money went to pay your landlord the rent. Still you survived … until 1845.

In August 1845 a fungus attacked the potatoes and it spread quickly over the country. The potatoes looked all right, but when you pulled them up they were black and rotten inside.

People went hungry and began to starve to death…

Asenath Nicholson – an American visitor said...

I was told of a cabin where in a dark corner lay a family of father, mother and two children lying together. The father was considerably rotted, whilst the mother had died last and had fastened the door so that their bodies would not be seen. Such family scenes were quite common. The cabin was simply pulled down over the corpses as a grave.

The countryside was emptied of its wildlife…

When the crop failed again in 1846, gangs of criminals formed known to the police as 'Ribbonmen'.

People would eat anything…

WE ATE THE BLOOD FROM A COW BAKED WITH VEGETABLES OR ANYTHING WE COULD FIND. DID YOU KNOW THAT YOU COULD TAKE TWO LITRES OF BLOOD FROM A LIVING COW BEFORE IT FALLS OVER?

SURE WE ATE THE DOGS FIRST, THEN THE DONKEYS, HORSES, FOXES, BADGERS, HEDGEHOGS AND EVEN FROGS. WE STEWED NETTLES AND DANDELIONS AND COLLECTED ALL THE NUTS AND BERRIES WE COULD FIND. THE PEOPLE ON THE COAST COULD EAT SHELLFISH BUT A LOT OF THEM WERE POISONOUS. MAYBE IT WAS BETTER A QUICK DEATH FROM POISONING THAN A SLOW ONE FROM HUNGER

MOST OF OUR CRIMES WERE STEALING FOOD AND MONEY. NOW THE PUNISHMENT FOR BEING CAUGHT WAS TO BE SENT TO AUSTRALIA … WHERE YOU'D BE WELL FED! SO IS IT ANY WONDER PEOPLE TURNED TO CRIME? ONE POOR WOMAN WAS CAUGHT STEALING FROM A FIELD. WHEN THE POLICE WENT TO HER HOUSE THEY FOUND A POT BOILING WITH A FEW ROTTEN SPUDS AND A DOG IN IT

The 'Colleen Bawn'

The Victorians loved bloodthirsty plays and the Irish enjoyed them as much as anyone. Helpless girls murdered by Victorian villains were always popular.

Colleen Bawn was the most famous Irish girl of the 1800s because a play was written about her. To be honest that's not her name, it's a description of her. The words mean 'lovely girl'. The play *Colleen Bawn* by the Dublin writer Dion Boucicault was hugely popular in Britain and America. It was a 'melodrama', full of sentimental nonsense, dreadful villains and innocent young women. Ever so popular in the days before *Coronation Street* and *Eastenders*.

What the Victorian audiences loved most of all was that it was based on a true and gruesome Irish murder. Here's a two-minute version for you to perform in your drama lesson to a shocked teacher.

THE CLOBBERED COLLEEN

CAST:

The 'Colleen Bawn' – 16-year-old Ellen Hanley – a Limerick farmer's lovely daughter

John Scanlon – Ellen's villainous boyfriend, a posh army officer

Stephen Sullivan – Scanlon's boatman and partner in crime

Scene 1 - A boathouse on the edge of the Shannon River

Loud music. Enter Scanlon and Sullivan. Loud boos!

Scanlon: It is just a year since I married Ellen, you know!

Sullivan: I know, boss. I was there! I dressed up as a priest and pretended to marry you to her! It was a good trick was that!

Scanlon: But now I am bored with her! I want to go to England and mix with the rich and elegant people. I cannot take a simple peasant girl like Ellen with me!

Sullivan: So what you gonna do, boss?

Scanlon: Tell her that the marriage was a fake! Tell her you were not really a priest. Tell her we are no longer married and that I am leaving her.

Sullivan: She'll not like that, boss.

Scanlon: Then she'll have to lump it.

Sullivan: Ah, but what you did was against the law! If she tells the constable you'll be arrested and go to prison for a long time. They may even transport you to Australia!

Scanlon: Then if she refuses to let me go you will have to kill her! I'll distract her. You smash her over the head with this gun. Row her out into the middle of the river, tie rocks to her feet and dump her. Then we'll be free.

Sullivan: Here she comes now!

Scanlon: Then hide! When I say the word, kill her.

Sullivan: What word?

Scanlon: The words 'Colleen Bawn'!

Sullivan hides. Soft music. Ellen enters

Ellen: Ah, John, my love. I'm so afraid. Why must we meet in this gloomy place?

Scanlon: 'Tis gloomy news I have to tell you!

Ellen: Oh, John! I feel a cold hand of fear clutching at my heart. What news?

Scanlon: The priest that married us was not a priest – he was some vile impostor. We thought that we were married. We were not.

Ellen: *(Almost swooning in a dead faint, clutches at Scanlon)*

Alas, the shame! My father would die of grief if he knew I was living with you and not married! We must find a true priest and marry at once.

Scanlon: I'm going away to England. We'll marry when I return.

Ellen: How long, my love?

Scanlon: A year or five!

Ellen: *(Cries out).* Five years! I will not let you go!

Scanlon: Then you must die, my Colleen Bawn!

Sullivan steps out from his hiding place. The gun is raised. Dramatic music. Blackout. A scream. A crash. Silence. Curtain falls.

On 6 September 1819, Ellen's body was washed up on the shore of the Shannon estuary near the village of Croom. Scanlon was hunted and found hiding in a hay barn, after a soldier prodded a bale of hay with his bayonet.

He was arrested and sent for trial at Limerick. Most people believed that a gentleman would never be convicted of killing a peasant. But Scanlon was found guilty and was hanged at Gallows Green in March 1820.

There was a story that the horses at first refused to pull his cart to the scaffold, because he was a gentleman!

His boatman, Stephen Sullivan was also hanged. He'd actually murdered the girl – smashing her skull with a gun – after drinking a bottle of whisky to give himself the courage. But Scanlon died because he gave the order.

Ellen was buried at Burrane churchyard, County Clare. And she still is!

WORKING BRITS

In the early 1800s the most dangerous and dirty job of all was coal mining. A mine inspector said...

Mining gives more ways of dying than any other job.

Men and women went underground for up to 16 hours a day. The more they dug out the more they were paid.

If a husband and wife were down the mine then what happened to the children? They couldn't afford to send them to school so they took them underground.

By the age of five the coal-covered kids were given a job as a 'trapper'. A trapper's job was to sit by the doors in the tunnels and open them every time a coal truck came along.

Easy? You could do that! Except...

- It was very dark and you had to listen for the trucks coming – if you failed to open the door, it would smash and you'd be in trouble.
- You were paid a penny a day – but if you bought a candle then it cost a half-penny a day ... so most trappers sat in the dark.
- You were out of bed at 4 a.m. to start work and you worked all day. If you fell asleep it could be a disaster.
- There were no toilets down there. You did what you had to do in a corner of the tunnel – and so did everyone else. Poo!

Here are the top ten ways to die in a mine – which would you prefer?

1. CRUSHED

If that tunnel collapses you are crushed like a worm under a wheel.

Note: In 1873 James Morrow (age 8) fell asleep while trapping. A coal truck sliced off his leg. James had a wooden leg fitted and went back down the mine a few months later. A roof collapsed and crushed him to death soon after. Not a lucky boy.

2. DROPPED

The lift rope snaps and drops you to the bottom of the pit shaft.

3. GASSED

A deadly gas called 'mine damp' can kill you and you can't even smell it.

Note: Miners took canaries down the mine. If the canary fell off its perch it had been gassed. Time to get out before the gas gets you next.

4. PLOPPED

You fall out of the lift.

5. EXPLODED

If you take a candle to light your way it can set off the mine-damp gas.

Note: On Wednesday, 8 September 1880, at Seaham (County Durham) more than 160 lives were lost in an explosion. Yet another 83 men died in another explosion at Seaham in 1951. You'd have thought things would get better.

6. BLOCKED

Stones fall out of the lift shaft as you wait at the bottom.

7. TRAPPED

If a mine shaft was blocked you were trapped and died slowly as the air ran out.

Note: At Earsdon (Northumberland) in 1862 the lift machine collapsed and trapped 204 men and boys. That was the only way out. They all died. William Gledson was 71 years old. John Armstrong was just 10. He died alongside his father.

8. ZAPPED

You are caught in an explosion of gunpowder that is used to loosen the coal.

9. DROWNED

Sometimes a thunderstorm could flood the pit and drown you before you could get out.

Note: In 1925 miners at the Montagu Pit in Newcastle dug through rock straight into an old flooded mine. 38 died. A map of the old mine would have helped them to avoid it. They didn't have a map. A piece of paper that would have saved 38 lives.

10. SQUISHED

Run over by a coal truck in a dark tunnel.

Cosher Bailey

Britain banned slavery in 1807. But many British workers were almost as badly off as slaves. The workers were so poor that children had to go to work from the age of seven. The Welsh worked for powerful 'iron-masters' and coal owners. Rich and ruthless men – usually English.

One iron-master at Nantyglo was called Crawshay Bailey – but his workers gave him the nickname 'Cosher'. Bailey was so hated that he had to build his family little fortresses in case the oppressed workers revolted.

Cosher Bailey decided he wanted one of these new steam train things and he would drive it himself. He drove his train along the Aberdare Valley in 1846. He set off into a tunnel – and the tall chimney on his engine jammed against the roof. The Welsh workers were so happy to see his disaster they wrote a funny song that they still sing today – 'Cosher Bailey's engine'.

1 Cosher Bailey had an engine,
It was always wanting mending,
And according to the power,
She could do four miles an hour

CHORUS:
Did you ever see, did you ever see,
Did you ever see, such a funny thing before?

2 Cosher bought her second-hand,
And he painted her so grand,
When the driver went to oil her,
Man, she nearly bust her boiler

3 Oh the sight it was heart-rending,
Cosher drove his little engine
And he got stuck in the tunnel,
And went up the blooming funnel

4 On the night run up from gower,
She did twenty mile an hour,
As she whistled through the station, man,
She frightened half the nation

5 Yes, Cosher Bailey he did die,
And they put him in a coffin,
But alas, they heard a knocking,
Cosher cried, 'I'm only joking.'

Wicked work

Many poor Scots tried to make a living by weaving. New machines made weaving faster and easier. But the new factories made life worse for the workers, not better.

WIN!
A BOWL OF PORRIDGE
NEXT WEEK

BULLY BOSS? BAD PAY? BRUTAL CONDITIONS? TOUGH!
IT'S ALL IN A DAY'S WORK SAYS OUR EMPLOYMENT EXPERT SNOOTY McSNOB

OUR CAREERS SECTION HAS HUNDREDS OF HORRIBLE JOBS

WEAVER WILSON PAYS PRICE

James Wilson, the sixty-year-old rebel leader, was brutally executed yesterday. The weavers' leader was fastened to a wooden sledge and dragged to a scaffold in front of the law courts in Glasgow. The old man wore an open-fronted shirt over his white prison uniform and white gloves. His mysterious travelling companion wore a black mask and carried an axe.

Last week Wilson was found guilty of treason. In April he had marched from the Lanarkshire village of Strathaven at the head of a small group of rebels. Wilson was armed with a rusty old sword and his followers had poor weapons. When they arrived in Glasgow they found the city was quiet and there was no support. They were easily arrested and brought to trial.

The judge sentenced him to suffer the ancient form of execution like William Wallace – to be hanged, drawn and quartered. A crowd of 20,000 gathered to watch the gruesome spectacle and there was a large guard of Dragoon soldiers to prevent trouble.

Wilson was hanged and died bravely. He was then cut down and beheaded with a single stroke of the axe. The executioner held up the white-haired head and cried, 'Behold the head of a traitor,' as was the old custom. The crowd jeered and hissed in disgust, crying, 'Shame!' and 'Murder!'

Some of the soldiers fainted at the sight. It was decided to spare his corpse the disgrace of being cut into quarters. He was thrown into a pauper's grave in Glasgow but his niece had the body dug up and returned to the churchyard in his Strathaven home.

Wilson's supporters have been distributing handbills telling his true sad story and saying, 'May the ghost of the murdered Wilson haunt the pillow of his cruel judge.'

Next week the rebels Baird and Hardy will go to a similar death in Stirling. Isn't it time Scotland gave up this barbaric punishment? No man deserves to die the way Wilson died. The judge called him a 'miserable and sinful creature'. Many poor Scots will see him as a martyr for a free Scotland.

Child cheats

Want to make some dishonest money? Of course you don't. But if you DID then here are some tips from villainous Victorian children you must NOT try at home…

THE SHIVERING DODGE

The shivering dodge was a favourite of 'Shaking Jemmy'. He went on shivering so long he couldn't stop himself – even when he was in a warm house.

THE LUCIFER DODGE

You can get your little friends to gather up the matches and try it again … and again…

THE TEA AND SUGAR DODGE

This dodge could earn up to 18 shillings in one morning when many working men didn't make ten shillings a week.

THE BIRD-BREAD DODGE

THE SCALDRUM DODGE

If looking ill doesn't help then pretend to choke on a piece of dry bread. Take money to get ale to wash the dry bread from your throat.

If everything fails then try this really disgusting one…

It is best if the bread is covered in maggots. Do NOT shake them off before you eat the bread – after all they make a nice bit of meat in your sandwich.

THE TERRIBLE 20TH CENTURY

If Britain had a Horrible History before 1901, when Queen Victoria died, then it was about to get a whole lot worse. TWO massive worldwide wars killed millions – and, for the first time, Brit women and children were killed in their own homes with bombs.

TERRIBLE TIMELINE

1901
Old Vic dies age 81. The family line up to kiss the dead queen's hand goodbye. Yeuch!

1912
Titanic ship launched in Belfast, Northern Ireland. They say it's unsinkable. Then ... the unthinkable. It sinks! 800 women, children and millionaires are first to the lifeboats but 1500 die a chilly death.

1914
The Great War with Germany starts. Very bloody. A newspaper reports, 'Cheer after cheer from the crowds greeted the news that the Mother Country (Britain) had declared war against Germany.' Four 'bloody' years later they will be cheering that it's all over.

Frightful First World War

The British joined the French to fight against the Germans. The Scottish soldiers often fought in kilts ... which terrified the Germans.

Both sides sat in muddy trenches facing each other a hundred yards apart. From time to time one side climbed out and marched across to attack the other. They were easy to shoot down with machine guns. Millions died.

A British Sergeant wrote a poem that sums it up...

You stand in a trench of vile stinking mud,
And the bitter cold wind freezes your blood.
Then the guns open up and the flames light
  the sky,
And, as you watch, rats go scuttling by.

The men in the dugouts are quiet for a time,
Trying to sleep midst the stench and the slime.
The moon is just showing from over the Hill,
And the dead on the wire hang silent and still.

A sniper's bullet wings close to your head,
As you wistfully think of a comfortable bed.
But now a dirty blanket has to suffice,
And more often than not, it is crawling with lice.

Haig and his mob keep well in the Rear,
Living in luxury, safe in old St Omer,
Flashing red tabs, brass and ribbons galore,
What the hell do they know about fighting a War?

1918

Great War ends. Just when you think it's a safe world to live in ... Spanish Flu strikes. The war kills 8.5 million. Spanish flu kills 20 million in just two years!

1921

An 'Irish Free State' created in south of Ireland while Ulster, in the north, stays part of Britain. That should be peace, but in fact it leads to 80 years of trouble.

1932

The Great Depression. Three million Brits out of work. Teachers get a pay cut to help the government save money. (Heh! Heh!)

1939

Prime Minister Chamberlain announces, 'This country is now at war with Germany.' Again. This time enemy bombers will wreck Britain in raids that are known as 'The Blitz'. Britain is led by Prime Minister Winston Churchill from 1940.

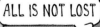

TOP SECRET

WOEFUL SECOND WORLD WAR: WONDERS TO WIN THE WAR

During World War II some people come up with wonderful ideas to help Britain win the war. Here are a few of them. But are they true?

1 DESTROY GERMANY'S OIL SUPPLIES

• The Germans get much of their fuel from Romanian oil fields. If the oil wells can be destroyed then German tanks, aeroplanes and ships will run out of fuel and become useless. Of course the oil fields are well defended.

• Send in a team of British commandos disguised as firemen. Give them fire engines that are exact copies of the Romanian Fire Brigade machines.

• Get the Royal Air Force to drop one or two fire bombs on the Romanian oil wells. When the fires start send in the British Commando fake-firemen. They can spray the fires with hoses, but more bombs would be mixed with the water-jets. The more they pour on the wells the more they will destroy!

2 NOBBLE THE NORWEGIANS

• Send in a small force of highly trained men to Norway. Keep the Germans so busy defending Norway that they can't defend Germany.

• Design a special three-man snow-sledge that can travel round Norway planting bombs.

• Of course the Germans would suspect a strange snow-sledge so it will have to be disguised. Disguise it as a hut and put a sign on that would keep out all curious German soldiers. The sign will say, 'Officers' Toilet. For Colonels only.'

3 FREEZE THE FOE

• Mix water and wood pulp then freeze it. You have an incredibly tough material called 'Pykrete'. Bullets and bombs just bounce off it and it doesn't melt very easily.

• Build a fleet of aircraft-carrier ships and troop-carrying ships out of Pykrete. Sail straight into enemy ports – their bombs and bullets can't stop you. Block the enemy harbours with Pykrete blocks so their ships can't get out.

• Spray their docks with Pykrete until they freeze up and leave the enemy navy helpless. Send sprayers into Germany to freeze up the railways and the factories until Germany has to give up and surrender.

Answers: **All TRUE**

1 This idea is planned but never carried out.

2 Trials are begun to build the snow-sledges, but too late to be of any use in the war.

3 Pykrete (invented by Geoffrey Pyke) really works. The British navy are so excited that Admiral Mountbatten catches Winston Churchill in his bath and drops a lump of Pykrete in. It doesn't melt. Germany is defeated before the Pykrete fleet is built.

1945

End of war with Germany. British people thank Mr Churchill by throwing his party out of power. The war may be over but not the suffering. Food is short, people queue for bread and small shares (or 'rations') of things like clothes and petrol, sweets and meats.

1969

Start of modern 'Troubles' in Northern Ireland when Catholics and Protestants riot. Violence grows as both sides start to use guns.

1982

Britain goes to war with Argentina over who owns the Falkland Islands. The average age of the soldiers is 19.

1993

Horrible Histories are invented and life for young Brits suddenly gets a whole lot better!

1997

The Labour party wins the British General Election and suddenly Prime Minister Tony Blair declares...

1998

Wales gets its own government, The National Assembly and Northern Irish people get their own government too ... is this end of Britain? Looks like it because...

1999

Scotland's Parliament opens. And only poor little English left without a parliament. Guy Fawkes would be pleased.

EPILOGUE

The English, the Irish, the Scots and the Welsh hardly ever fight these days. So it's time to put away those scrapping saints and find a new saint for the whole of Britain.

But George *didn't* slay a dragon, he only tamed it and made it Christian. And, if he existed at all, then he was a crook who sold rotten bacon to the Roman army. Britain doesn't need him!

But David was so strict his monks hated him. They even tried to murder him. You don't want a saint who's as popular as poison.

Except Patrick was *not* the first man to take the Christian religion to Ireland. Anyway he was a Welshman.

Andrew never visited Britain, of course. Some say his bones were pinched from the Romans and taken to Scotland. But that's just a legend.

No, Britain needs a new saint. A hero to take it through the 21st century.

Who should it be?

Tell you what ... pick your own. Here are a fab forty of some hopeless heroes the islands have seen.

I know who I would choose. Who do you think?

GREAT BRITISH LOSERS

Britain has had many heroes and heroines in its history. But a lot of them were losers. Brits just seem to love a brave little loser better than a big bully winner! Here are a top ten from each country...

 ## ☠ ENGLAND ☠

1 CARATACUS
DIED AD 54
Led the tribes in southern Britain against the Roman invasion ... and lost. Betrayed by Queen Cartimandua of northern England. The rat! Taken to Rome to be executed but spared because he was so brave. Phew!

2 BOUDICA
DIED AD 61
Fought against the Roman settlers – massacred thousands of them in cold blood. Then lost. Went off and probably poisoned herself. Horrible heroine and tough old boot. May be buried under Platform 8 at King's Cross station. Urgh!

3 KING ARTHUR
DIED 539 ... MAYBE
When the Romans left the Saxons started to arrive. The Brits fought back and could have been led by a king called Arthur. Finally defeated at the Battle of Camlann. The hero becomes a legend who will return when Britain is in danger. Hurry!

4 HAROLD GODWINSSON
1020–1066
Fought against the Norman invader, William the Conqueror, at the Battle of Hastings in 1066 – and lost. Wounded with an arrow in the eye which did not bother him for long because he was hacked to pieces soon after. Ouch!

 ### 5 RICHARD THE LIONHEART
1157–1199
Fought in the Crusades but was captured on his way home. Cost England a fortune to get him back. Then he goes off to fight the French where he is killed with a poisoned arrow in the neck. A funeral is cheaper than a ransom. Clink!

6 WAT TYLER
DIED 1381
Led the Peasants' Revolt against the terrible taxes of the time. After murdering lots of posh people in London he was stabbed and dragged off to have his hair cut with an axe across the neck. The poor peasants lost – but not as much as Wat. Thunk!

7 RICHARD III
1452–1485
Murdered his way to the English throne killing two little princes in the Tower of London (probably). Then along came Welsh invader, Henry Tudor, and Richard went down fighting at the Battle of Bosworth. End of the Middle Ages. Slam!

8 GUY FAWKES
1570–1606
Joined the plot to blow up King James. The King was making life miserable for the Catholics and Guy wanted to fight back. He was caught on 4 November 1605, tortured and executed by hanging, drawing and quartering. Slice!

9 DICK TURPIN
1705–1739
A highwayman, cattle thief, smuggler and thug. A cruel criminal who became a sort of hero when a storybook was written about him. He was betrayed by his old school teacher – typical. He was caught and hanged. Cccct!

10 NED LUDD
ABOUT 1810
The Industrial Revolution brought in machines to do the work of men and women. The poor workers starved. Ned Ludd led a revolution against the revolution by smashing the machines and the army won. Loser Ludd. Crunch!

☠ IRELAND ☠

1 SAINT PALLADIUS
DIED 431
The Pope sent Palladius to Ireland to teach the Irish about Christianity. A tough job among cruel people. Patrick went across a year later and did a better job. It is Patrick who became patron saint of Ireland. Loser Palladius, forgotten. Who?

2 KING FEDELMID
820–47
The king and bishop of Cashel at a time when the Vikings were raiding his people. But foul Fedelmid does a better job than the Vikings and burns more churches than they ever could. In the end he is killed – by the monks! Hallelujah!

3 Brian Boruma
941–1014

Irish kings were always squabbling. But Brian was the biggest and best. He could bring peace by beating the Vikings at the battle at Clontarf. No more arguments. Brian wins! Hooray. But he also gets himself killed. Oooops!

4 King Dermot
died 1171

The Irish were fighting one another as usual. King Dermot had a bright idea ... invite the Normans from England to help him! The Normans came and conquered – then decided to stay and rule over daft Dermot's land. Ohhhh!

5 Silken Thomas
died 1534

Silken Thomas was given the name because his soldiers wore silk on their helmets. He tried to rebel against Henry VIII's rule but lost. Went over to England to be executed. A long way to go to die. Sigh!

6 Grace O'Malley
died 1603

Grace was the pirate queen of western Ireland – she cropped her hair short and was nicknamed 'Granuaille' in Irish, which means 'Baldy'. She was caught, of course, but Elizabeth I said she'd let her off if she gave up pirating. Splash!

7 Wolfe Tone
1763–1798

Leader of the Society of the United Irishmen. He invited the French across to help throw out the English rulers. But the invasion failed and lots of people died. Wolfe was thrown into prison but beat the hangman by cutting his own throat. Swipe!

8 Robert Emmet
1778–1803

Guess what? Another rebel, another loser. The Irish had seen what happened to Wolfe Tone so they weren't so keen to follow Emmet. Only 80 mates helped him raid Dublin Castle – with one ladder. Crowded! Lost and hanged. Drop!

9 Daniel O'Connell
1775–1847

A leader who wants a peaceful end to British rule. But it doesn't work any better. When a monster meeting is called the police tell him to call it off – and he does. The violent rebels will leave him to form the 'Young Ireland' group. Flop!

10 William Smith O'Brien
1803–1864

After a few years of terrible famine the 'Young Ireland' try to rebel. In the battle of Widow McCormack's Cabbage Garden two rebels die and O'Brien is arrested. But the losers find a new weapon – the idea of a free Ireland. O'Brien is freed. Oooh! O'Bother.

1 ST DONAN
DIED **617**
Daring Donan set out to convert the wild Scots to Christianity. He is doing a really, really good job then makes a silly mistake. He gets into an argument with a band of Pict warriors about some sheep and the Picts kill him. Baa!

2 KING MACBETH
DIED **1057**
Will Shakespeare wrote a play about Macbeth and made him out to be a villain who murdered an old King Duncan. In fact he beat a young King Duncan in battle, fair and square. He was then defeated in battle. Smash!

3 ALEXANDER III
DIED **1286**
He rode his horse along a cliff top at night and they slipped over the cliff. This caused a terrible problem because it left Scotland without a king and the evil English moved in to take over. Some say Alex was pushed over by enemies? Neigh!

4 WILLIAM WALLACE
1272–1305
Scottish rebel who led his men against the English invaders. He won a battle at Stirling Bridge in 1297 – the first time the Scots had beaten an English invader. But he was betrayed by a Scot, taken to London where his guts were pulled out and burned. Sizzle!

5 ROBERT THE BRUCE
1274–1329
The famous story says a spider in a cave taught this rebel to keep going to victory. Robert smashed the English at Bannockburn in 1314 and wins freedom for Scotland in 1328. Then he does a foolish thing and dies in 1329. Crown down. Clunk!

6 KATE DOUGLAS
1437
Assassins came to murder James I. To give James a chance to escape, the Queen's servant, Kate Douglas, barred the door with her arm. The attackers rammed the door and shattered her arm in two. The King hid in a sewer but was found and murdered. Snap!

92

7 KING JAMES IV
1473–1513
Henry VIII of England went off to fight the French, so brave James decided to invade. He reckoned without Henry's Queen Catherine. She sent an army to meet him and beat him at Flodden Field. James went down fighting. Scrunch!

8 MARY QUEEN OF SCOTS
1542–1587
Fought against her Scots enemies and lost. She went to see her cousin Elizabeth I of England for safety. But Elizabeth kept her safely in prison for 19 years. When Mary plotted to escape (and kill Liz) she was executed with three messy chops. Slop!

9 BONNIE PRINCE CHARLIE
1720–1788
Wanted to rule Britain as King James III. The Scots flocked to fight for him. They managed to beat the English a few times but, in the end, Charlie's weak and starving army were blown to pieces at the Battle of Culloden. Charlie lived on, the dream didn't. Boom!

10 ROBERT BURNS
1759–1796
Robbie was Scotland's greatest hero poet ever. But he never made any money from it so he took a job trying to catch smugglers. Instead he caught a chill while having a drunken sleep under a hedge. It killed him at the age of 36. Brrrr!

☠ WALES ☠

1 SAINT DAVID
AROUND 500
A monk and the patron saint of Wales. But he wasn't so popular when he was alive. He was such a harsh bishop that his monks tried to poison him just to get a bit of peace. But a dog and a crow ate the poison and died. Flump!

2 PRINCE CADWALLON
DIED 633
Smashed the Saxons and massacred women and children. Had the chance to take over Britain for the Welsh but wasted it. Instead he went round robbing and killing. In the end the English killed him in a battle at Hexham. Chance gone. Pfffft!

93

3 RHODRI THE GREAT
DIED **878**

The Welsh found a hero to defend them: Rhodri the Great who became ruler of most of Wales by the 850s. And he united Wales against the Viking invaders and sent them packing. But the English beat him in battle. Same old story. Groan!

4 GRUFFYDD AP LLEWELYN
DIED **1063**

Murdered his way to the top of the Welsh tree. Wales was one country at last – for just seven years. But his enemies caught up with him and he was killed in his own castle. His head was cut off and sent to Harold the warrior leader of England. Snick!

5 MADOG AB OWAIN
AROUND **1172**

The Normans marched in and took over a lot of Wales. So sensible Madog sailed as far away as he could go. It's said he reached America 300 years before Columbus. So America should be part of Wales today. But Madog didn't claim it. Tut!

6 LLEWELYN THE GREAT
DIED **1282**

A history of the time said... 'He ruled his enemies with sword and spear.' He put his brothers in prison and made himself prince of Wales. But he got into a silly fight with an English soldier and lost. His head was sent to London. Drip!

7 OWAIN GLYNDWR
DIED **1415**

Owain din't want to be a rebel. But he got into an argument over some land and formed an army to settle it. It turned into war and for a while Owain was winning. But as the English and his Welsh enemies closed in he vanished. Whoosh!

8 HENRY TUDOR
1457–1509

The Welshman invaded England and threw Richard III off the throne. For a hundred years the Tudor family would rule England till Elizabeth I, the last Tudor, popped off. The Welsh ruled Britain! But Henry Tudor did nothing for the Welsh people. Tush!

9 SIR HENRY MORGAN
1635–1688

This pirate was a hopeless sailor who blew up his own ships or ran them onto rocks. But he somehow managed to beat the Spanish in the Caribbean and the King made Henry Governor of Jamaica where he drank himself to death aged 53. Glug!

10 DIC PENDERYN
DIED **1831**

The Welsh led the way in a Brit struggle to give ordinary men the vote. (But not women). In a scrap with the army in Newport a soldier was stabbed in the leg. Dic Penderyn was hanged even though he didn't do it. Huh!

INTERESTING INDEX

Hang on! This isn't one of your boring old indexes. This is a horrible index. It's the only index in the world where you will find brutal body-snatchers, dodgy dragons, poo and all the other things you really HAVE to know if you want to be a horrible historian. Read it and creep.

Aborigines (Australian people) 62

Angles, angry 13, 24

Anglo Saxon Chronicle 27

archaeologists, archaic 9–10, 16

Aughrim, battle of 58

Bannockburn, battle of 39, 43, 92

barrows, bone-chilling 9–10

Berserkers (Viking warriors) 19

Black Agnes (Scottish countess) 43

Black Death (dreadful disease) 40

Blitz, blazing 85

body bits
　boiling 30
　burning 9, 60–1, 65, 92
　cut off/up 25, 32, 57, 60, 68–71, 81
　eating 27, 52–5, 59
　preserved 16–17

body-snatchers, brutal 71

Bonnie Prince Charlie (Stuart prince) 62, 64–5, 93

Boruma, Brian (Irish king) 25, 91

Bosworth, battle of 41, 46, 90

Boucicault, Dion (Irish writer) 76

Boudica (British queen) 12, 15, 89

British Isles 5, 11

British Museum 16

Bronze Age, barmy 10

Bruce, Robert the (Scottish king) 39, 42–3, 92

Burke and Hare (Scottish murderers) 71

Burns, Robbie (Scottish poet) 54–5, 93

caber, tossing the 36

Cadwallon (Welsh prince) 93

Calgacus (Caledonian leader) 16

Cavaliers (Charles I's supporters) 56

Celts, cut-throat 13, 16–17, 24, 28, 35

Charles I (British king) 56

Charles II (British king) 57

Chartists, crushed 74

children
　cheating 82–3
　coal-mining 78–80
　cut up 23
　eating 54, 59
　lowly 31
　rules for 45
　selling 53–4

cholera (dreadful disease) 73

Churchill, Winston (British leader) 85–7

Civil War, crucial 56

Claudius (Roman emperor) 12, 14

Colleen Bawn (Irish play) 76–7

Crimean War, crazy 73

criminals, cruel 68–72

Cromwell, Oliver (English protector) 22–3, 57

Culloden, battle of 62, 64–5, 93

Dark Ages, dreadful 24–7, 68

deer antlers, digging with 10

Dermot (Irish king) 29, 91

Douglas, Kate (Scottish heroine) 44, 92

dragons, dodgy 5–6, 88

Druids (Celtic wizards) 16–17

Edward I (English king) 38, 41–2

Elizabeth I (English queen) 47–8, 91, 94

England 5, 11–13, 18–19, 22, 24, 27, 38, 46–7, 56, 58, 61–2, 64, 89–91, 93–4

English Channel 7–8, 15

famine, foul 48, 53, 59, 62, 73–5, 91

Fawkes, Guy (English plotter) 56, 87, 90

feudal system, funny 31

First World War, frightful 84–5

Flodden, battle of 51, 93

French Revolution 63, 66

Fussell's Barrow, building 10

games, grim 35–7

garroting, gruesome 72

George I (British king) 62

Georgians, gory 62–7

Glencoe Massacre 58

Glyndwr, Owain (Welsh leader) 41, 94

Gordon, George (English lord) 62–3

Great Britain, invented 58, 63

Great Charter (Magna Carta) 38

Great Depression, grim 85

Great Fire of London 57

Great Plague (dreadful disease) 57

Great War, grisly 84–5

Hadrian (Roman emperor) 13, 16, 52

haggis (Scottish meat pudding) 54–5

Harold (English king) 18–20, 89, 94

Hastings, battle of 18–19, 89

henges, horrible 10–11

Henry VII (English king) 46, 90, 94

Henry VIII (English king) 46–51, 91

historians, horrified 15-17, 61
Homo Erectus (early human) 7
Hundred Years War 39-40
hunting, horrific 37
hurley hacket (Scottish sledging) 36
hurley (Irish hockey) 35

Ireland 5, 7-8, 11, 14, 22-3, 40, 47, 54, 57-8, 63, 66-7, 73, 85, 90-1

Jacobite rebels (Stuart supporters) 62, 65
James IV (Scottish king) 51, 93
James VI/I (Scottish/English king) 47-8, 56, 60-1, 90
Joan (Scottish queen) 44

Lindow Man (preserved body) 16-17
Llewelyn the Great (Welsh ruler) 94
Ludd, Ned (English rebel) 90

Mary of Gueldres (Scottish queen) 44
Mary, Queen of Scots 47-8, 93
Matilda (English empress) 28-9
Middle Ages, measly 33, 38-41, 45
miners, miserable 63, 78-9
Morgan, Henry (Welsh pirate) 94
Murphy, John (Irish priest) 66-7

Napoleonic Wars 63
Neanderthals (early humans) 7
Neolithic Age, nauseating 10
New Grange (Irish monument) 8
Nicholas, Jemima (Welsh heroine) 20-1
Nightingale, Florence (British nurse) 73
Normans, nasty 18-19, 25, 27-9, 41, 89, 91, 94

O'Brien, William Smith (Irish leader) 73, 91
Odo (Norman bishop) 30

Peasants' Revolt 38, 40, 89
Picts, perilous 13, 24, 92
poo 78
prehistoric people, puzzling 7-11
recipes, revolting 9, 52-5, 59, 74-5

Rhodri the Great (Welsh ruler) 94
Ribbonmen (Irish gang) 75
Richard III (English king) 41, 46, 90
rituals, revolting 9-10
Romans, rotten 8, 12-14, 18, 27, 52, 88-9
Roundheads (Parliament's supporters) 56-7

St Andrew (patron saint of Scotland) 6, 88
St David (patron saint of Wales) 6, 88, 93
St George (patron saint of England) 5, 88
St Patrick (patron saint of Ireland) 5, 24, 88, 90
Saxons, savage 13-14, 24-5, 27-8, 52-3, 68, 89, 93
schools, suffering 45, 58, 73
Scotch Cattle (Welsh gang) 63
Scotland 5-6, 8, 11-12, 14, 24-5, 28-9, 36, 38, 41-2, 46, 48, 51, 54, 56-8, 60-1, 64, 80-1, 87, 92-3
Second World War, woeful 21, 86
Shakespeare, William (English playwright) 56, 92
Spanish Armada 47
Spanish Flu 85
spelling, scrappy 45
sports, special 34-7
Stephen (English king) 28-9
Stone Age, surprising 8-9
Stonehenge (English monument) 8, 11
Strongbow (Norman earl) 32
Stuarts, slimy 40, 56-62, 64
surgeons, sick 71
Swift, Jonathan (Irish writer) 54

Tacitus (Roman writer) 14, 16
taxes, tortuous 38-40
timelines, troublesome 7-8, 24-5, 28-9, 38-41, 56-8, 62-3, 73, 84-5, 87
Tone, Wolfe (Irish leader) 63, 66-7, 91
torture, terrifying 46, 48, 60-1, 66, 68-70, 74, 90
trains, invented 63, 73, 80
Tudors, terrible 41, 46-51, 56, 58, 70, 94
twentieth century, turbulent 84-7
Tyler, Wat (English peasant) 40, 89

Victorians, vile 72-7
Vikings, vicious 10, 19, 25, 52, 90-1, 94

Wales 2, 5, 8, 11, 16, 24, 40-1, 47, 56-8, 63, 74, 80, 87, 93-4
Wallace, William (Scottish leader) 38, 42, 81, 92
warriors, women 20-1, 43-4
Wars of the Roses 40-1, 46
weavers, worried 80-1
Widow MacCormack's Cabbage Garden, battle of 73, 91
William the Conqueror (Norman invader) 18-19, 28, 30, 32, 89
William and Mary (British king/queen duo) 58
Wilson, James (Scottish weaver) 81
witches, worse for 11, 60-1, 71